P9-DUG-392

IDENTIFYING

CACTI

The new compact study guide and identifier

CACTI

The new compact study guide and identifier

Charles Glass, Clive Innes and Marcus Schneck

CHARTWELL
BOOKS, INC.

A QUINTET BOOK

Published by Chartwell Books, Inc.
A Division of Book Sales, Inc.
114 Northfield Avenue
Edison, New Jersey 08837

This edition produced for sale in the U.S.A., its
territories and dependencies only.

ISBN 0–7858–0373–4

This book was designed and produced by
Quintet Publishing Limited
6 Blundell Street
London N7 9BH

Creative Director: Richard Dewing
Designer: James Lawrence
Project Editors: Diana Steedman, Alison Bravington
Editor: Maggie O'Hanlon
Illustrator: Danny McBride

The material in this publication previously appeared in: *Cacti* by Marcus Schneck
and *The Illustrated Encyclopedia of Cacti* by Clive Innes and Charles Glass.

Typeset in Great Britain by
Central Southern Typesetters, Eastbourne
Manufactured in Hong Kong by Regent Publishing Services Ltd
Printed in China by Leefung-Asco Printers Ltd

CONTENTS

HOW TO USE THIS BOOK

The introduction describes the main features of the family Cactaceae and gives general advice on cultivation. The identifier section consists of individual entries for a wide cross-section of cactus species. Each entry is illustrated and gives concise details of the main characteristics of the species, its origin and its cultivation requirements. The symbols accompanying each entry convey the essential information at a glance.

SHAPE

 Columnar

 Globular

 Padded/ Jointed

 Clustering

 Pendent

 Leaf-like

 Sprawling/ Trailing

 Climbing

FLOWERING PERIOD

 Mid-winter

 Mid-spring

 Mid-summer

 Mid-autumn

 Late winter to early spring

 Late spring to early summer

 Late summer to early autumn

 Late autumn to early winter

MINIMUM TEMPERATURE

 7°C (45°F)   15–16°C (59–61°F)

 10°C (50°F)   18°C (64°F)

 13°C (55°F)   19°C (66°F) and over

LIGHT

 Good but indirect light   Direct sunlight

 Partial shade   Full shade

FLOWERING TIME

 Diurnal

 Nocturnal

COMPOST

 Slightly acid compost   Enriched mineral compost

 Standard cactus compost   Calcareous compost

7

INTRODUCTION

There are over 2,000 members of the Cactaceae, nearly all originating from North and South America, although a few belonging to the genus *Rhipsalis* are native to Africa. Several American species have been introduced to other continents where they have become naturalized.

These succulent plants occupy habitats ranging from humid, tropical jungles to the driest deserts, and from just above sea-level, where the salt spray collects on the spines, beads and drops to the soil, to the tallest mountains, where they may occasionally be covered by snow. Rela-

tively few live in true desert, i.e. where rainfall is less than 240mm (1in) per year, but a surprising variety has taken advantage of the tiny nooks and crannies available on rocky slopes.

SHAPE AND SIZE

Cacti species are extremely variable in size; the smallest, when mature, are the size of a thimble while the tallest of the tree-like species may reach 24m (80ft) in height. They are also extremely variable in shape and habit but can be broadly categorized as follows.

1. Globular. This large group can be subdivided according to the shape and arrangement of the spines and the presence or absence of tubercles or a cephalium.

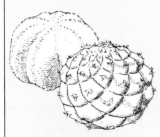

(a) Few or no spines (*Astrophytum, Aztekium, Blossfeldia, Echinocereus, Lophophora, Turbinicarpus*).

(b) Fine spines (*Acanthocalycium, Echinomastus, Epithelantha, Escobaria, Frailea, Gymnocalycium, Mammillaria*).

(c) Straight, short spines (*Echinocereus, Neolloydia, Neoporteria, Pediocactus, Pygmaeocereus, Sclerocactus, Thelocactus, Uebelmannia*).

(d) Prominent spines (*Ancistrocactus, Coryphantha, Denmoza, Echinocactus, Echinocereus, Echinofossulocactus, Echinopsis, Eriosyce, Ferocactus, Gymnocactus, Homalocephala, Lobivia, x Lobivopsis, Trichocereus*).

(e) Spines arranged in a comb-like formation (*Buiningia, Pelecyphora*).

(f) Flat or prominent tubercles, often scale-like (*Ariocarpus, Ferobergia, Leuchtenbergia, Neowerdemannia, Obregonia, Ortegocactus, Pelecyphora, Strombocactus*).

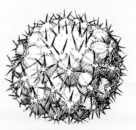

(g) With a woolly or spiny crown (*Copiapoa, Matucana, Notocactus, Oroya, Parodia, Weingartia*).

(h) Prominent cephalium (*Discocactus, Melocactus*).

2. Columnar. Within this
basic shape, which is
common to many cacti, there
are a number of variations.

(a) Bushy (*Armatiocereus,
Austrocephalocereus,
Bergerocactus,
Calymmanthium, Leocereus,
Mammillaria, Neoraimondia,
Opuntia, Pereskia,
Pereskiopsis, Quiabentia,
Stenocereus, Subpilocereus,
Tacinga, Thrixanthocereus,
Wilcoxia*).

(c) Of robust, tree-like
habit (*Browningia,
Carnegiea, Facheiroa,
Neobuxbaumia, Neodawsonia,
Pachycereus, Rauhocereus,
Stetsonia*).

(b) Erect or semi-
prostrate (*Arrojadoa,
Arthocereus, Borzicactus,
Cereus, Coleocephalocereus,
Corryocactus, Echinocereus,
Pachygerocereus*).

(d) Of slender, tree-like
habit (*Cereus, Dendrocereus,
Escontria, Eulychnia,
Jasminocereus, Lasiocereus,
x Myrtillocactus, Polaskia,
Pseudopilosocereus,
Pterocereus, Samaipaticereus,
Siccobaccatus, Stenocereus,
x Stenomyrtillus,
Weberbauerocereus*).

(e) Semi-climbing
(*Mirabella, Monvillea*).

(h) Spiny (*Acanthocereus,
Borzicactus,
x Myrtgerocactus,
Trichocereus*).

(f) With a particularly
short column
(*Ancistrocactus, Astrophytum,
Austrocactus, Borzicactus,
Brachycereus, Echinocereus,
Echinomastus, Escobaria,
Lobivia, Mammillaria,
Neolloydia, Setiechinopsis*).

(i) Densely spined
(*Borzicactus, Haageocereus,
Hildewintera*).

(g) Woolly or hairy
(*Cephalocereus, Cipocereus,
Cleistocactus, Espostoa,
Neobinghamia, Oreocereus,
Pilosocereus*).

(j) With a prominent
cephalium (*Backebergia,
Buiningia, Lophocereus,
Micranthocereus,
Staphanocereus, Vatricania*).

3. Clustering.

(a) Cushion-like
(*Coryphantha, Mammillaria, Rebutia, Sulcorebutia*).

(b) Group-forming
(*Echinocereus, Epithelantha, Escobaria, Ferocactus, Gymnocalycium, Pygmaeocereus*).

(c) Sparse (*Chamaelobivia, Matucana, Sulcorebutia*).

(d) Sprawling and spreading
(*Maihuenia, Maihueniopsis, Tephrocactus*).

4. Pendent. The shape of the stems is the distinguishing characteristic.

(a) Segmented
(*Acanthorhipsalis, Rhipsalidopsis, Rhipsaphyllopsis, Schlumbergera*).

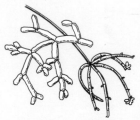

(b) More or less tubular
(*Hatiora, Lepismium, Rhipsalis*).

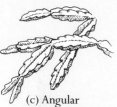

(c) Angular
(*Aporoheliocereus, Aporophyllum, Borzicactus, Heliocereus, Pfeiffera, Selenicereus*).

(d) Elongated (*Aporocactus, Erythrorhipsalis*).

(e) Leaf-like (*Discocactus, Lymanbensonia, Nopalxochia*).

5. Padded or jointed (*Opuntia, Pterocactus, Tephrocactus*).

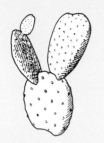

6. Climbing (*Hylocereus, Seleliocereus, Selenicereus, Strophocactus*).

7. Leaf-like.

(a) Broadly leaf-like (*Cryptocereus, Disocactus, Epicactus, Epiphyllum, Nopalxochia, Wittiocactus*).

(b) With segmented stems (*Lepismium, Rhipsalis, Schlumbergera*).

8. Sprawling or trailing with stems that are:

(a) Leafy (*Pereskia*).

(b) Very thin (*Peniocereus, Weberocereus, Wilcoxia, Wilmattea*).

(c) Firm, sprawling (*Borzicactus, Echinocereus, Haageocereus, Loxanthocereus, Pseudoacanthocereus, Stenocereus*).

(d) Slender, strongly spined, sprawling (*Eriocereus, Harrisia, Heliocereus, Nycticereus, Trichocereus*). Some genera exhibit such diversity that they may fall into more than one group.

13

SHAPES OF CACTUS SPINES

Radial spines, no centrals

Fine radial spines with
a single central spine

Stout, curved
central spine

Conical, stout spines

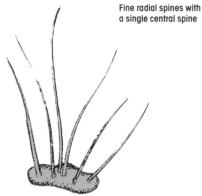

Bristly, hair-like spines

Protruding, hooked
central spine

Stout, banded, curved
central spine

Comb-like, pectinate spines

Needle-like,
protruding spines

Paper-like, flexible, flat spines

ANATOMY

The plant itself consists of a swollen stem and leaves that have been reduced to spines or scales. The stem surface has taken on many of the functions of the leaf and, in some instances, has a leaf-like appearance, while the centre acts as a water-storage organ. Stems generally have ribs or tubercles which bear felted growing points called areoles. Some cacti have a densely woolly, bristly "head", or cephalium, from which the flowers are produced. New growth and spines, and usually the flowers, develop from the areoles, which sometimes bear a tuft of bristly hairs, known as a glochid. The spines often appear in clusters, consisting of one or more central spines and a number of radial spines, varying in shape according to species (see p.14).

FLOWERS

Flowers are hermaphrodite in nearly all cases. Most are diurnal, i.e. they only open fully during daylight hours. Should they last for several days they may either remain open all the time or close during the hours of darkness. Most of the columnar cacti, and some of the globular ones, are nocturnal, or night-flowering. Tightly closed during daylight hours, the flowers start to open in the late afternoon or early evening and remain open all night, closing again in the early morning. Flowering season varies according to species. Pollination is effected by insects, or even by birds and bats, and a seed-filled fruit is produced.

SEED DISPERSAL

In some species, the fruit dries and cracks open, releasing the seeds; in others the fruit is moist and fleshy and the seeds are dispersed via the excrement of the birds and animals which feed upon it. Many cacti also propagate vegetatively, by producing offsets.

CULTIVATION

Grow cacti in clay or plastic containers just large enough to accommodate the plant comfortably. For mixed plantings, ensure that the selected species have the same cultivation requirements.

Compost

All cacti require an open-textured soil for free drainage and the circulation of air. Standard cactus compost usually consists of equal parts sterilized loam, shredded sphagnum peat and sharp gritty sand, with a slow-release fertilizer. If a soil-less compost is used, add 1 part washed gritty sand to every 2 parts compost.

Cacti from certain habitats may have additional requirements. Spiny or woolly desert cacti will benefit from the addition of limestone gravel in the ratio 1 part gravel to 6 parts compost. Forest cacti require a richer, more acid soil and so a small quantity of granulated, decomposed leafmould or cow manure should be added to the standard compost (about ¼ in bulk of the peat content). For cacti from sloping rocky habitats, where decomposed plant material and minerals are washed from the rocks, the compost should consist of 1 part sterilized loam, 1 part shredded peat and 2 parts sharp gritty sand or fine gravel, enriched with 1 part granulated, decomposed leafmould to 3 parts compost.

Light

Desert species require strong, direct sunlight for strong growth, successful flowering and strong spines whereas rainforest and jungle cacti do best in shaded conditions. Many others, especially the smaller ones and juveniles, grow in the shade of surrounding vegetation and thus prefer partial shade. Nevertheless, regardless of their individual requirements, all cacti need a certain amount of light for photosynthesis to occur.

Temperature and humidity

For most cacti grown indoors, normal room temperature will suffice during summer and a minimum of 5°C (40°F) in winter. Desert cacti, however, require a minimum of 8–10°C (46–50°F) throughout their winter dormancy and species from extremely hot climates, e.g. *Melocactus* and *Discocactus*, require a minimum of 15°C (59°F). In spring, a daytime maximum of 22–27°C (70–80°F) will promote flowering and growth in most desert cacti. Jungle and rainforest cacti will accept much the same temperature ranges as their desert counterparts except during bud formation and at the onset of flowering; at these times, temperatures should never be allowed to fall below 10°C (50°F). As they are accustomed to humid conditions in their natural habitats, regular overhead misting with tepid rainwater will prove beneficial to these plants.

Watering and feeding

Water with extreme care because overwatering can lead to black rot. During the growing season, until mid- to late autumn, water in the early morning or late evening; soak the compost well and allow it to dry out before watering again. In hot, dry weather, a gentle spraying with water in the evening will simulate the formation of dew. During the dormant period, most desert species will survive without water, although plants kept in a warm, centrally heated room should be moistened occasionally, and jungle and rainforest species should be kept moist. Resume watering in early spring, increasing the quantity and frequency as summer approaches. Without proper feeding, growth will be retarded and flowers will be of poor quality, if they develop at all. Apply a comprehensive fertilizer, i.e. one containing nitrogen, potassium and potash plus essential trace elements, in diluted form every 3–5 weeks during the growing season. Alternatively, use fertilizer specially formulated for cacti.

Propagation

Most cacti can easily be propagated by cuttings and offshoots. To obtain a cutting, take a sharp knife and remove a portion of the stem at its narrowest joint. Offshoots should be removed in midspring and during summer. Allow to rest in a warm,

dry place until the wound has healed before planting in a highly porous medium, e.g. coarse sand, perlite or vermiculite. Seeds should be planted in small, shallow containers, preferably plastic, that can be covered by glass. After an initial drenching, keep the soil moist by immersing the containers, and maintain at temperatures between 21°C and 32°C (70°F and 90°F). The emerging plant should be protected from direct sunlight.

PROPAGATION BY CUTTINGS

Slice through the stem with secateurs or a sharp knife.

Place cuttings in a warm, dry place until a callus forms.

Insert cuttings into compost, just deep enough to keep them upright.

When cuttings show signs of growth, remove and pot them on.

ACANTHOCALYCIUM VIOLACEUM

Solitary, more or less globular cactus with a finely spined, dull green stem bearing about 15 ribs.

SIZE 20cm (8in) tall, 13cm (5in) in diameter.

AREOLES White-felted; set along the ribs.

SPINES Yellowish-brown. 12 or more slender radials. 3–4 slightly longer centrals.

FLOWERS Bell-shaped, 7.5cm (3in) long and 6cm (2½in) in diameter, and pale violet. Produced from or near the apex.

FLOWERING TIME Diurnal, in summer.

ORIGIN Argentina (Cordoba).

CULTIVATION Grow in standard cactus compost, in full sun and in an airy position, at a minimum winter temperature of 7°C (45°F).

ACANTHOCEREUS HORRIDUS

Semi-erect, multi-branched, columnar cactus. The spiny, dark green stems, which are 10cm (4in) thick, have 3 wing-like ribs with scalloped margins.

SIZE Variable.

AREOLES Set 3–6cm (1¼–2½in) apart along the ribs.

SPINES As many as 6 radials, up to 1cm (½in) long, 1 or 2 thick brownish centrals, about 5cm (2in) long, maturing to grey.

FLOWERS About 20cm (8in) long, and white with greenish-brown outer segments.

FLOWERING TIME Nocturnal, in summer.

ORIGIN Guatemala.

CULTIVATION Grow in standard cactus compost, in full sun, at a minimum temperature of 13°C (55°F).

ANCISTROCACTUS UNCINATUS

Short, columnar cactus with a flattened apex. The bluish-green stem has up to 13 protruding, straight ribs, bulging at the areoles.

SIZE 20cm (8in) tall, 7cm (3in) in diameter.

AREOLES White-felted and surrounded by yellowish hairs; set along the ribs.

SPINES 8 thick white radials. 1 or 2 centrals, one of which is hooked at the tip.

FLOWERS Bell-shaped, up to 2.5cm (1in) long, and burnt orange with white-edged petals. Produced from the apex.

FLOWERING TIME Diurnal, in midsummer.

ORIGIN USA (Texas), Mexico (northern to central).

CULTIVATION Grow in standard cactus compost with added grit, in full sun, at a minimum temperature of 10°C (50°F).

APOROCACTUS MARTIANUS

Creeping or pendent cactus with many elongated, cylindrical stems. Up to 1m (3ft) long and to 2cm (¾in) in diameter, these have 8 low ribs.

SIZE Variable.

AREOLES Cream-felted: set 6–10mm (¼–½in) apart along the ribs.

SPINES 6–8 thin yellowish radials. 2 or more, rather bristle-like yellowish centrals.

FLOWERS Somewhat funnel-shaped, 4cm (1½in) long and about 6cm (2½in) in diameter, and red. Produced along the stems.

FLOWERING TIME Diurnal, in early summer.

ORIGIN Mexico (Oaxaca).

CULTIVATION Grow in full sun, in standard cactus compost, at a minimum temperature of 13°C (55°F).

ARIOCARPUS TRIGONUS

Globular cactus with a single, greyish-green stem bearing many semi-erect tubercles. These are triangular, 5cm (2in) long and 2.5cm (1in) broad at the base, with a flat, unfurrowed upper surface and acute tips.

SIZE 10–15cm (4–6in) in diameter.
AREOLES Set at the tips of the tubercles.
SPINES None.
FLOWERS About 5cm (2in) across, and yellowish. Produced from the axils of the tubercles.
FLOWERING TIME Diurnal, in midsummer.
ORIGIN Mexico (Nuevo Leon, Tamaulipas).
CULTIVATION Grow in a gritty, enriched compost; in full sun, at a minimum temperature of 13°C (55°F). Do not water in winter.

ARMATOCEREUS CARTWRIGHTIANUS

Bushy, freely branching, columnar cactus. The branches consist of dull green joints, 15–60cm (6–24in) long and 8–15cm (3–6in) in diameter, with 7–8 prominent ribs.

SIZE 3–5m (10–15ft) tall.
AREOLES Large and brown; set along the ribs.
SPINES About 20, whitish or dark brownish, 1–2cm (½–¾in) long, maturing to 12cm (5in) long.
FLOWERS 7–8cm (3in) long, with white inner petals and reddish outer petals.
FLOWERING TIME Nocturnal, in summer.
ORIGIN Ecuador, northern Peru.
CULTIVATION Grow in standard cactus compost; in partial shade, at a minimum temperature of 13°C (55°F).

ARROJADOA RHODANTHA

Erect, often climbing cactus, frequently branching from the base. The dark green stems are more or less cylindrical, 2–4cm (¾–1½in) thick, and have 10–14 low-set ribs. They continue to grow through the brown-woolly, reddish-brown-bristly cephalium to form another flowering apex the following year. Very occasionally, an unusual form occurs in which the cephalium becomes cristated with bristles and wool running laterally on the stem. The fruit is round and purple.

SIZE 2m (6ft) tall.

AREOLES Light-brown-felted at the base; set about 1cm (½in) apart along the ribs.

SPINES Yellowish at first, becoming brown. About 20 radials, 5–6 centrals, all 1–3cm (½–1¼in) long.

FLOWERS Tubular, 3–3.5cm (1¼–1½in) long and 1–1.2cm (½in) in diameter, and purplish-pink. Produced from the cephalium.

FLOWERING TIME Diurnal, in early summer.

ORIGIN Brazil (Bahia, Minas Gerais).

CULTIVATION Grow in standard cactus compost, in full sun, at a minimum temperature of 13°C (55°F).

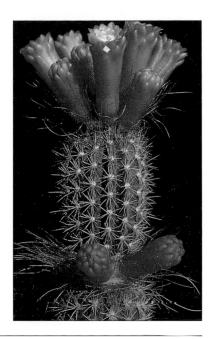

ASTROPHYTUM ASTERIAS
SEA URCHIN CACTUS

Solitary, globular cactus, distinctly flattened at the apex. The purplish-brown stem, speckled throughout with roundish white scales, has 6–8 almost totally flat ribs with straight grooves between them.

SIZE 5cm (2in) tall, 10cm (4in) in diameter.

AREOLES Conspicuous and white-felt-covered; set about 6mm (¼in) apart along the ribs.

SPINES None.

FLOWERS Daisy-like, about 3cm (1¼in) long and 4cm (1½in) across, yellow and slightly reddish in the throat, although this tends to be disguised by the pollen. Produced from the centre of the apex.

FLOWERING TIME Diurnal, in early summer.

ORIGIN Mexico (Tamaulipas).

CULTIVATION Grow in standard cactus compost, in full sun, at a minimum temperature of 7°C (45°F).

ASTROPHYTUM MYRIOSTIGMA

BISHOP'S CAP

Globular to cylindrical cactus with a basically green stem. This is totally covered with minute whitish scales that obliterate the ground colour and has 4–8 very pronounced ribs.

SIZE 10–20cm (4–8in) in diameter.

AREOLES Brownish and woolly; set very close together, or even touching, along the ribs.

SPINES None.

FLOWERS Daisy-like, 4–6cm (1½–2½in) long and 6cm (2½in) in diameter, and yellow, sometimes with a red centre. Produced from the centre of the apex.

FLOWERING TIME Diurnal, in summer.

ORIGIN Mexico (central and northern). Found at high altitudes (over 2000m/6565ft).

CULTIVATION Grow in standard cactus compost, in full sun, at a minimum temperature of 10°C (50°F).

AUSTROCEPHALOCEREUS DYBOWSKII

Erect, columnar cactus with several felt-covered stems growing straight upwards from the base. Each has 20–28 low ribs densely covered with fine spines and matted yellowish wool. The white-woolly cephalium may extend for 20–60cm (8–24in) downwards from the apex.

SIZE 2–4cm (¾–1½in) tall, 8–10cm (3–4in) in diameter.

AREOLES Closely set along the ribs.

SPINES Many short, fine radials, mostly hidden by felt. 2–3 yellowish centrals, 2–3cm (¾–1¼in) long.

FLOWERS Bell-shaped, 4–6cm (1½–2½in) long, and whitish. Produced from the cephalium.

FLOWERING TIME Nocturnal, in summer.

ORIGIN Brazil (Bahia).

CULTIVATION Grow in standard cactus compost, in full sun, at a minimum temperature of 15°C (59°F).

AZTEKIUM RITTERI

A unique species of flattened, globular cactus, often sprouting from the base to form compact groups. The olive-green stem has 9–11 ribs, about 1cm (½in) high and 8mm (⅜in) broad, with smaller protrusions between them. It is circled horizontally by irregular, linear indentations that fan out progressively more towards the bottom, giving the appearance of scaling.

SIZE 5cm (2in) in diameter.

AREOLES Minute and white-felted; closely set along the ribs.

SPINES 1–4 flat, papery and twisted, up to 4mm (⅛in) long, and soon falling.

FLOWERS 1cm (½in) long and 8mm (⅜in) wide, and white or pink. Produced from new areoles in the centre of the apex.

FLOWERING TIME Diurnal, in summer.

ORIGIN Mexico (Nuevo Leon). Found on stony, slaty slopes.

CULTIVATION Grow in standard cactus compost, in full sun, at a minimum temperature of 10°C (50°F).

BACKEBERGIA MILITARIS

Robust, columnar cactus, branching into an almost tree-like canopy. The stems are up to 12cm (4½in) in diameter and have 5–11 slightly protruding ribs. The apex of the stem is covered by a dome-like cephalium of orange-brown bristles.

SIZE 6m (20ft) tall.

AREOLES Off-white-felted; set along the ribs.

SPINES Greyish and 1cm (½in) long. 7–13 radials. 1–4 centrals.

FLOWERS Bell-shaped, 7cm (3in) long and 4cm (1½in) in diameter, and orange-red, opening to creamy white. Produced from the centre of the cephalium.

FLOWERING TIME Nocturnal, in summer.

ORIGIN Mexico (Guerrero, Michoacan).

CULTIVATION Grow in standard cactus compost, in full sun, at a minimum temperature of 13°C (55°F).

BLOSSFELDIA LILIPUTANA

Very small, slightly flattened, globular cactus with a greyish-green stem that has no ribs.

SIZE 1cm (½in) in diameter.

AREOLES Sparsely woolly.

SPINES None.

FLOWERS Open-petalled, up to 1cm (½in) in diameter when fully open, and whitish-yellow. Produced from the centre of the apex.

FLOWERING TIME Diurnal, in midsummer.

ORIGIN Argentina, Bolivia.

CULTIVATION Grow in standard cactus compost, in full sun, at a minimum temperature of 13°C (55°F).

BORZICACTUS SAMAIPATAMUS

Initially erect cactus, later becoming pendent, with elongated, vertical, bright green stems, up to 1.5cm (½in) long and 3–5cm (1¼–2in) in diameter. These branch from the base and have an even number (14–16) of evenly spaced ribs. The fruit is red, round and covered with felt.

SIZE Variable.

AREOLES Brownish; set 3–4mm (⅛in) apart and staggered in relation to those on adjacent ribs.

SPINES 13–22 slender and yellowish-brown, 0.4–3cm (⅛–1¼in) long.

FLOWERS Tubular, curved, 4–6cm (1½–2½in) long, and deep red with paler edges and lighter-coloured stamens. The flower tube is covered with hairs and scales. Produced around the curve of the apex.

FLOWERING TIME Diurnal, in summer.

ORIGIN Bolivia (Santa Cruz).

CULTIVATION Grow in standard cactus compost, in moderate to full sun, at a minimum temperature of 10°C (50°F).

B RACHYCEREUS NESIOTICUS

Rather short, clustering, columnar cactus with greenish stems that are densely spined and bear 13–16 ribs.

SIZE 30–60cm (12–24in) tall.

AREOLES Pale brownish and 2.5mm (⅛in) wide; set along the ribs.

SPINES 40 or more, initially brown, becoming grey, up to 3cm (1¼in) long.

FLOWERS 4–6.5cm (1½–2½in) long and 2.5–3cm (1–1¼in) in diameter, with narrow white petals. Produced from the sides of the stems.

FLOWERING TIME Nocturnal, in summer.

ORIGIN Galapagos Islands.

CULTIVATION Grow in slightly calcareous compost, in full sun, at a minimum temperature of 15°C (59°F).

B ROWNINGIA HERTLINGIANA

Columnar cactus with a rounded apex. The bluish-green stems, which tend to branch with maturity, have 18 or more ribs with wedge-shaped indentations between the areoles.

SIZE Up to 8m (25ft) tall, 30cm (1ft) in diameter.

AREOLES Prominent and grey-felted; set along the ribs.

SPINES Yellowish-grey with brown tips. 4–7 radials. Up to 3 centrals, to 8cm (3in) long. More spines develop as the plants mature.

FLOWERS Tubular with an upward curve, about 5cm (2in) in diameter, with white inner petals, purplish externally. There are many scales along the tube.

FLOWERING TIME Nocturnal, in summer.

ORIGIN Peru (Mantaro Valley).

CULTIVATION Grow in standard cactus compost containing a little lime, in full sun, at a minimum temperature of 13°C (55°F).

B U I N I N G I A   A U R E A

Short, columnar cactus, branching freely from the base to form clumps. Individual stems are dull green and 7–10cm (3–4in) in diameter, with 10–16 ribs. A pseudocephalium, composed of white wool and bristles, develops laterally.
SIZE 60cm (24in) tall.
AREOLES Set along the ribs.
SPINES Golden yellow. 10–15 radials, 1–2cm (½–¾in) long. 1–4 centrals, 5–7cm (2–3in) long.
FLOWERS Very small and pale yellowish-green. Produced from the pseudocephalium.
FLOWERING TIME Nocturnal, in summer.
ORIGIN Brazil (Minas Gerais).
CULTIVATION Grow in standard cactus compost, in full sun, at a minimum temperature of 13°C (55°F).

C A R N E G I E A   G I G A N T E A
SAGUARO

Erect, tree-like, columnar giant, branching at about 2.2m (7ft) and repeatedly from that point, both from the main stem and branches. Each dark green branch has 12–24 vertical ribs. The elliptical red fruit is edible. This slow-growing cactus is familiar from "Western" films.
SIZE 14m (46ft) tall, 65cm (26in) in diameter.
AREOLES Set about 2cm (¾in) apart along the ribs.
SPINES 12 or more brownish-grey radials, 1–2cm (½–¾in) long. 3–6 thicker brownish centrals.
FLOWERS Funnel-shaped, about 12cm (5in) long and across, with whitish inner petals, green externally. Produced from the stem tips.
FLOWERING TIME Diurnal, in early summer.
ORIGIN Mexico (Sonora), USA (Arizona, California).
CULTIVATION Grow in standard cactus compost, in full sun, at a minimum temperature of 10°C (50°F).

CEPHALOCEREUS SENILIS

OLD MAN CACTUS

Columnar cactus, frequently branching from the base and covered with blue-grey hair towards the apex. The grey-green stem has 12–30 low, rounded ribs and a cephalium develops in maturity. The fruit is red and covered in cream hairs.

SIZE 15m (50ft) tall, 40cm (16in) in diameter.

AREOLES Closely set along the ribs.

SPINES 20–30 hair-like white radials, 6–12cm (2½–5in) long. 1–5 centrals, 1.2–5cm (½–2in) long.

FLOWERS Trumpet-shaped, about 8.5cm (3¼in) long and 7cm (3in) in diameter, and whitish-yellow. Produced from the cephalium, along one side of the stem near the apex.

FLOWERING TIME Nocturnal, in summer.

ORIGIN Mexico (Guanajoto, Hidalgo).

CULTIVATION Grow in standard cactus compost, in full sun, at a minimum temperature of 13°C (55°F).

CEREUS AETHIOPS

Erect, slender, rarely branching, columnar cactus with a dark blue stem, later becoming dark green, with 8 ribs bearing small warts.

SIZE 2m (6ft) tall, 3–4cm (1¼–1½in) in diameter.

AREOLES Almost black; set about 1.5cm (½in) apart along the ribs.

SPINES Black. 9–12 radials, up to 1.2cm (½in) long. 2–4 centrals, up to 2cm (¾in) long.

FLOWERS Up to 20cm (8in) long, with white or pale pink inner petals and greenish-brown outer petals. Produced from the sides of the stem.

FLOWERING TIME Nocturnal, in summer.

ORIGIN Argentina (Mendoza).

CULTIVATION Grow in standard cactus compost, in full sun, at a minimum temperature of 10°C (50°F).

C EREUS CHALYBAEUS

Tall, columnar cactus with bluish to dark green branches, few in number, 5–10cm (2–4in) thick, and bearing 5–6 deeply furrowed ribs.
SIZE 3m (10ft) tall.
AREOLES Set about 2cm (¾in) apart along the ribs.
SPINES Blackish. 7–9 radials, up to 1.4cm (½in) long. 3–4 slightly longer centrals.
FLOWERS Saucer-shaped, up to 20cm (8in) across, white internally and reddish externally. Produced on the sides of the branches.
FLOWERING TIME Nocturnal, in summer.
ORIGIN Argentina, Brazil.
CULTIVATION Grow in standard cactus compost, in full sun, at a minimum temperature of 10°C (50°F).

C EREUS PERUVIANUS

Tall, slender, branching, columnar cactus with bluish to dull green stems bearing 5–8 protruding ribs that are acutely furrowed and notched where the areoles appear.
SIZE 3–5m (10–15ft) tall, 10–25cm (4–10in) in diameter.
AREOLES Tan-felted; set about 2cm (¾in) apart along the ribs.
SPINES 4–7 brown radials, about 1cm (½in) long. 1 reddish-brown central, up to 2cm (¾in) long.
FLOWERS Tubular, about 16cm (6in) long, and white with greenish-brown outer petals. Produced near the apex.
FLOWERING TIME Nocturnal, in summer.
ORIGIN Argentina, Brazil (very uncertain).
CULTIVATION Grow in standard cactus compost, in full sun, at a minimum temperature of 10°C (50°F).

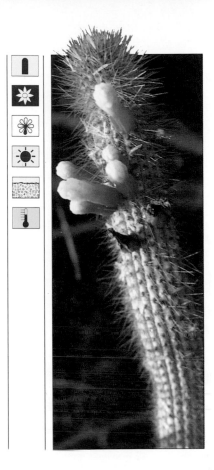

CLEISTOCACTUS BROOKEI

Semi-erect or somewhat sprawling, columnar cactus. The greenish stems, about 50cm (20in) long and 4–5cm (1½–2in) in diameter, have about 25 ribs.

SIZE Variable.

AREOLES Greyish-brown; set along the ribs.

SPINES 30–40 greyish-white or slightly yellowish, 4–9mm (⅛–⅜in) long.

FLOWERS Tubular, about 5cm (2in) long, and mostly carmine red. Produced from the sides of the stems.

FLOWERING TIME Diurnal, in late summer.

ORIGIN Bolivia (Santa Cruz).

CULTIVATION Grow in standard cactus compost, in full sun, at a minimum temperature of 13°C (55°F).

CIPOCEREUS PLEUROCARPUS

Fairly short, columnar cactus with dull greenish stems, each with 10–16 ribs, 3–5mm (⅛–¼in) high.

SIZE Stems about 3cm (1¼in) in diameter.

AREOLES Brownish-white; set along the ribs.

SPINES 8–11 brown radials, up to 1cm (½in) long. 4 or more prominent centrals, up to 2.5cm (1in) long.

FLOWERS Tubular, about 5cm (2in) long, creamy white and slightly scented. Produced from the side of the stem near the apex.

FLOWERING TIME Nocturnal, in midsummer.

ORIGIN Brazil (Serra do Cipo, Minas Gerais).

CULTIVATION Grow in standard cactus compost, in full sun, at a minimum temperature of 13°C (55°F).

COLEOCEPHALOCEREUS BRAUNII

Semi-sprawling, columnar cactus recently discovered by Horst, Pereira and Braun. The bright green stems have 12 or more prominent, notched ribs. The cephalium, consisting of yellowish spines and wool, appears when plants reach a height of 15cm (6in). The fruit is purple.

SIZE 1m (3ft) tall.

AREOLES Pale brownish; set along the ribs.

SPINES Yellowish.

FLOWERS Open-petalled and greenish-white. Produced from the cephalium.

FLOWERING TIME Nocturnal, in summer.

ORIGIN Brazil (Espiritu Santo).

CULTIVATION Grow in standard cactus compost, in full sun, at a minimum temperature of 13°C (55°F).

COPIAPOA HYPOGAEA

Solitary, globular cactus with a rounded apex set with white wool and fairly rough skin. The dull brownish-green stem has 10–14 slightly spiralled ribs regularly divided into tubercles.

SIZE 4–6.5cm (1½–2½in) in diameter.

AREOLES White-woolly; set in a slight depression at the tips of the tubercles.

SPINES 1–6 brownish, 2 4mm (¹⁄₁₆–⅛in) long, and soon falling.

FLOWERS Often bell-shaped, up to 3cm (1¼in) across and 2cm (¾in) long, and glossy yellow. Produced from the apex.

FLOWERING TIME Diurnal, in late summer.

ORIGIN Chile (Antofagasta).

CULTIVATION Grow in standard cactus compost, in good but indirect sun, at a minimum temperature of 10°C (50°F). Very careful watering is required.

CORYPHANTHA ANDREAE

NIPPLE CACTUS

Solitary, globular, prominently spined cactus that may become slightly columnar with maturity. The glossy, dark green stem is encircled by sharply protruding tubercles, 2cm (¾in) high and 2.5cm (1in) thick. The apex is slightly concave with a white-felt-covered centre.

SIZE 9cm (3½in) in diameter.

AREOLES The deep indentation extending from the areoles along the upper edge of each tubercle is white-felted.

SPINES About 10 yellowish-grey radials, up to 1.2cm (½in) long. 5–7 heavier, curved centrals up to 2.5cm (1in) long.

FLOWERS With widely spreading petals, up to 5–6cm (2–2½in) across, and bright yellow. Produced from the apex.

FLOWERING TIME Diurnal, in summer.

ORIGIN Mexico (Vera Cruz).

CULTIVATION Grow in standard cactus compost, in full sun, at a minimum temperature of 10°C (50°F).

CORYPHANTHA MACROMERIS VAR. RUNYONI

Densely clustering cactus with prominent spines. The small, cylindrical, greyish-green stems have rounded tubercles, 1–2cm (½–¾in) high.

SIZE Up to 50cm (20in) across (clusters).

AREOLES Felted.

SPINES Yellowish- to reddish-orange and up to 3cm (1¼in) long. 6–7 radials. 1–3 centrals.

FLOWERS Funnel-shaped, up to 5cm (2in) wide, and white flushed with pinkish-purple. Produced from the apex.

FLOWERING TIME Diurnal, in midsummer.

ORIGIN USA (eastern Texas).

CULTIVATION Grow in slightly calcareous compost, in full sun, at a minimum temperature of 10°C (50°F).

DENMOZA ERYTHROCEPHALA

Solitary, globular to elongated cactus with a greyish-green stem bearing 20–30 low, rounded ribs, deeply furrowed.

SIZE 1.5m (5ft) tall, 15–30cm (6–12in) in diameter.

AREOLES Brown when young, becoming white-woolly with flexible, hair-like bristles; set along the ribs.

SPINES 30 or more, reddish-brown, up to 6cm (2½in) long.

FLOWERS Tubular, up to 7.5cm (3in) long; the red petals are 1cm (½in) long and close together with protruding stamens, style and stigma.

FLOWERING TIME Diurnal, in summer.

ORIGIN Argentina (Mendoza).

CULTIVATION Grow in standard cactus compost, in full sun, at a minimum temperature of 10°C (50°F).

DISCOCACTUS CEPHALIACICULOSUS

Somewhat flattened, globular cactus. The stem has 13–18 ribs divided into prominent tubercles. The distinctive cephalium is covered in white wool and bears protruding reddish spines.

SIZE 13cm (5in) tall, 20–26cm (8–10in) in diameter.

AREOLES Set at the tips of the tubercles.

SPINES Horn-coloured becoming dark grey. Up to 6 radials, 3.7cm (1½in) long. Rarely, 1 central up to 2.5cm (1in) long.

FLOWERS Up to 4cm (1½in) long and about 3cm (1¼in) across, and white.

FLOWERING TIME Nocturnal, in summer.

ORIGIN Brazil (Goias).

CULTIVATION Grow in standard cactus compost, in full sun, at a minimum temperature of 16°C (61°F).

DISOCACTUS EICHLAMII

Pendent, epiphytic cactus with a slender, cylindrical stem. The many flattened branches, about 30cm (12in) long and 5cm (2in) wide, are slightly fleshy with scalloped margins.
SIZE Variable.
AREOLES Small; set along the branch margins.
SPINES None.
FLOWERS Slender and trumpet-like, about 6cm (2½in) long, and carmine red. Produced at the margins of the branches.
FLOWERING TIME Diurnal, in succession from late winter to early spring.
ORIGIN Guatemala.
CULTIVATION Grow in porous acid compost, in partial shade, at a minimum temperature of 15°C (59°F).

ECHINOCACTUS POLYCEPHALUS

Globular, sometimes elongated, prominently spined cactus that is solitary initially but later forms large clumps. The stems have 13–21 ribs.
SIZE 40–70cm (16–28in) tall, 18–25cm (7–10in) in diameter.
AREOLES Whitish-grey; set about 3cm (1¼in) apart along the ribs.
SPINES Reddish-brown, 4–8 somewhat flat, spreading radials, up to 5cm (2in) long. 4 centrals, 4–9cm (1½–3½in) long.
FLOWERS Tubular, 5–6cm (2–2½in) long, and yellow. Produced from the apex.
FLOWERING TIME Diurnal, in summer.
ORIGIN Mexico (Sonora), USA (California, Nevada).
CULTIVATION Grow in standard cactus compost, in full sun, at a minimum temperature of 10°C (50°F).

Echinocereus Knippelianus

Globular, almost oval cactus with a slightly concave apex. The very dark green stem bears 5–6 rounded ribs divided by broad furrows. Additional stems grow from the taproot to form a cluster.

SIZE 5cm (2in) or more in diameter.

AREOLES White-felted; set at widely spaced intervals along the ribs.

SPINES 1–3 short, bristle-like, curving and cream, up to 1.5cm (½in) long.

FLOWERS Funnel-shaped, about 4cm (1½in) long, and pink. Produced from areoles near the apex.

FLOWERING TIME Diurnal, in spring and early summer.

ORIGIN Mexico (Coahuila).

CULTIVATION Grow in standard cactus compost, in full sun, at a minimum temperature of 10°C (50°F).

Echinocereus Pectinatus

RAINBOW CACTUS

Solitary, globular or short, columnar cactus, with a curved apex, that branches from the base to form a cluster. The blue-green stem bears as many as 20 ribs that are wider at the base and almost completely covered by the comb-like arrangement of spines.

SIZE 15–20cm (6–8in) tall, 5cm (2in) in diameter.

AREOLES Protruding, round, cream-and-brown-felt-covered; set along the ribs, more closely at the apex.

SPINES 20–25 white and pink radials. 6 short cream centrals.

FLOWERS Funnel-shaped, opening very wide, up to 8cm (3in) in diameter, with a spiny tube about 6cm (2½in) long. Petals are shimmering pink and stamens are yellow. Produced around the apex.

FLOWERING TIME Diurnal, in summer.

ORIGIN Mexico.

CULTIVATION Grow in standard cactus compost, in full sun, at a minimum temperature of 10°C (50°F).

Echinocereus subinermis

Globular cactus becoming elongated and occasionally clustering. The dull green stem, about 15cm (6in) long and 7–9cm (3–3½in) thick, bears 5–9 prominent ribs with narrow furrows between them. Small clusters of stems may grow from the same root.

SIZE 15cm (6in) tall, 9cm (3¾in) in diameter.

AREOLES Small and grey-felted; set along the ribs.

SPINES 3–10 off-white radials, 4mm (⅛in) long. 1 greyish central, 7mm (¼in) long. Mature plants are almost spineless.

FLOWERS Open-petalled, about 9cm (3¼in) in diameter, and bright lemon yellow. Produced from stems that appear near the apex.

FLOWERING TIME Diurnal, in summer.

ORIGIN Mexico (central and northern states).

CULTIVATION Grow in standard cactus compost, in full sun, at a minimum temperature of 10°C (50°F).

Echinocereus triglochidiatus var. goniacanthus

CLARET-CUP CACTUS

Short, columnar cactus with a slightly flattened apex. The cylindrical, dull green stem, up to 6cm (2½in) in diameter, has 7–9 more or less acute ribs. Stems tend to grow in small clusters.

SIZE 20cm (8in) tall.

AREOLES Greyish-white-felted; set along the ribs.

SPINES 8 thick greyish-yellow radials, 1.5–2cm (½–¾in) long. 1 black-tipped yellowish central, about 6cm (2½in) long.

FLOWERS Open-petalled, 4–5cm (1½–2in) long, and vivid, yellowish-orange with creamy yellow stamens. Produced from tubes that emerge from the side of the stem.

FLOWERING TIME Diurnal, in summer.

ORIGIN USA (southern states).

CULTIVATION Grow in standard cactus compost, in full sun, at a minimum temperature of 10°C (50°F).

ECHINOFOSSULOCACTUS PHYLLACANTHUS

Solitary, prominently spined, globular cactus with a slightly flattened apex. The dark bluish-green stem has 30–35 thin, wavy-edged ribs.

SIZE 8cm (3in) in diameter.

AREOLES Set about 2.5cm (1in) apart along the ribs, staggered in adjacent rows.

SPINES Red to brown, 7 in all. Upper 3 are 4–8cm (1½–3in) long and flat. Others are slender and spreading.

FLOWERS Tubular, up to 2cm (¾in) long, and yellowish-white with a brownish-red throat. Produced from the centre of the apex.

FLOWERING TIME Diurnal, in late spring.

ORIGIN Mexico (Hidalgo).

CULTIVATION Grow in standard cactus compost, in full sun, at a minimum temperature of 10°C (50°F).

ECHINOMASTUS UNGUISPINIS

Solitary, globular cactus with a slightly flattened apex. The dark blue-green stem is prominently spined and has no ribs.

SIZE 12cm (5in) tall, 10cm (4in) in diameter.

AREOLES Large and white-woolly; scattered over the surface.

SPINES 25 whitish radials, up to 2cm (¾in) long. 4–8 thicker, slightly longer brownish centrals. Radials intertwine with those of adjacent areoles, covering the entire surface of the plant.

FLOWERS Bell-shaped, about 2.5cm (1in) long and 2cm (¾in) across, and deep reddish-brown with yellow stamens. Produced from the centre of the apex.

FLOWERING TIME Diurnal, in summer.

ORIGIN Mexico (Chihuahua, Zacatecas).

CULTIVATION Grow in permeable, slightly calcareous but enriched compost, in full sun, at a minimum temperature of 10°C (50°F).

ECHINOPSIS AUREA

More or less globular cactus, prominently spined and with a rounded apex. The dark green stem has 14–15 sharp-edged ribs separated by horizontal notches. Each stem tends to produce many offshoots at its base, forming substantial colonies.

SIZE 10cm (4in) tall, 6–7cm (2½–3in) in diameter.

AREOLES Tan-felted in young plants, naked in older plants; set about 1cm (½in) apart along the ribs.

SPINES 8–10 thin, pale brown radials, about 1cm (½in) long. About 4 blackish-brown centrals, up to 3cm (1¼in) long.

FLOWERS About 9cm (3½in) long and 8cm (3in) across, bright yellow on the inside and burnt orange on the outside. The tube is greenish-white and the stamens are cream. Produced from the sides of the stem.

FLOWERING TIME Diurnal, in summer.

ORIGIN Argentina (Cordoba).

CULTIVATION Grow in standard cactus compost, in full sun, at a minimum temperature of 10°C (50°F).

X EPICACTUS "SWEET ALIBI"

ORCHID CACTUS

This extremely fascinating cultivar has erect, broad, leaf-like pads growing from a central root. The margins of the pads are serrated.

SIZE Variable.

AREOLES Greyish-felt-covered; set on the edges of the pads.

SPINES None.

FLOWERS Funnel-shaped, 13–15cm (5–6in) in diameter at the perimeter, with slender, rose-cerise petals shading to a deeper colour at the outer edges and cream stamens. Produced from some of the areoles.

FLOWERING TIME Diurnal, in spring.

ORIGIN Produced by M. Monmonier of Ventura Gardens, USA.

CULTIVATION Grow in standard cactus compost, in indirect sun, at a minimum temperature of 10°C (50°F).

EPIPHYLLUM OXYPETALUM

Much-branching epiphyte with cylindrical stems and broad, flat, leaf-like branches, 10–12cm (4–5in) wide. The fruit resembles a plum.
SIZE Up to 3m (10ft) long.
AREOLES Naked, rarely bristly.
SPINES None.
FLOWERS Long, curving and tubular, 25–30cm (10–12in) long and 12cm (5in) across, with white petals.
FLOWERING TIME Nocturnal, in midsummer.
ORIGIN Brazil, Guatemala, Mexico, Venezuela.
CULTIVATION Grow in porous, enriched compost, in full shade and high humidity, at a minimum temperature of 13°C (55°F).

EPITHELANTHA MICROMERIS

BUTTON CACTUS

Unusual, globular cactus, solitary or group-forming, with a rounded but slightly concave, white-woolly apex. The thick-set green stem has spiralling rows of small tubercles set close together and is almost obscured by the heavy, tightly woven spines that tend to cover the whole surface. Offsets commonly grow from the base of the main stem. Red berries are produced at the base of the flowers.
SIZE 6cm (2½in) tall, 2.5–4cm (1–1½in) in diameter.
AREOLES Small; set at the tips of the tubercles.
SPINES Tufts of about 20, spreading and white, up to 2mm (¹⁄₁₆in) long.
FLOWERS Funnel-shaped, about 1cm (½in) across, and white or pale pink with a deeper coloured throat. Produced in clusters from the centre of the apex.
FLOWERING TIME Diurnal, in summer.
ORIGIN Mexico (Coahuila, Nuevo Leon), USA (Texas).
CULTIVATION Grow in calcareous compost, in full sun, at a minimum temperature of 10°C (50°F).

ERIOCEREUS JUSBERTII

Usually solitary cactus of slender. sprawling habit. The elongated, angular, dark green stems are 4–6cm (1½–2½in) thick and bear 5–6 broad, protruding ribs.

SIZE Variable.

AREOLES Yellow-felted; set 2cm (¾in) apart along the ribs.

SPINES 7 dark brown radials, 5mm (¼in) long 1–4 slightly longer black centrals.

FLOWERS Open-petalled, up to 15cm (6in) long and 18–20cm (7–8in) in diameter, with pure white inner petals and brownish-green outer segments. Produced from the sides of the stems.

FLOWERING TIME Nocturnal, in summer.

ORIGIN Argentina or Paraguay.

CULTIVATION Grow in standard cactus compost, in filtered sun, at a minimum temperature of 10°C (50°F).

ESCOBARIA CHAFFEYI

Solitary or clustering, finely spined, egg-shaped cactus with a rounded apex. The dark olive-green stem is covered with tubercles.

SIZE 12cm (5in) tall, 5–6cm (2–2½in) in diameter.

AREOLES White-felted; set at the tips of the tubercles.

SPINES Up to 20 bristly white radials, 6mm (¼in) long. Up to 3 slightly shorter brown-tipped centrals.

FLOWERS Open bell-shaped, about 1.5cm (½in) long and 1cm (½in) in diameter, and yellowish-white with a broad reddish-brown centre. Produced from the centre of the apex.

FLOWERING TIME Diurnal, in summer.

ORIGIN Mexico (Cedros, Zacatecas).

CULTIVATION Grow in standard cactus compost, in full sun, at a minimum temperature of 10°C (50°F).

ESCOBARIA MINIMA

Solitary or clustering cactus with a more or less egg-shaped, dark green stem. Conical tubercles, up to 2cm (¾in) long, are separated by bare grooves.
SIZE 2.5cm (1in) tall, 2cm (⅞in) in diameter.
AREOLES Set at the tips of the tubercles.
SPINES Pinkish becoming grey. 13–15 radials, about 3mm (⅛in) long. 3 centrals, about 6mm (¼in) long.
FLOWERS Open-petalled, about 2cm (¾in) long and 1cm (½in) in diameter, and rose pink with yellow stamens. Produced from the apex.
FLOWERING TIME Diurnal, in summer.
ORIGIN USA (Texas).
CULTIVATION Grow in standard cactus compost, in partial shade, at a minimum temperature of 10°C (50°F).

ESPOSTOA LANATA
OLD LADY CACTUS

Erect, columnar cactus with an almost tree-like canopy of stems branching from the upper trunk. Stems are 4–10cm (1½–4in) in diameter, rounded at the apex, with 18–28 rounded ribs. The dark green surface is mostly masked on younger areas with silky white hairs. These are noticeably thicker at the apex of each stem. The large, berry-like red fruit is 4–6cm (1½–2½in) in diameter.
SIZE 4m (12ft) tall, 15cm (6in) in diameter.
AREOLES White; set about 5mm (¼in) apart and alternating with those on adjacent ribs.
SPINES White or pale yellowish, often red and very short. Centrals are up to 8cm (3in) long and point directly outwards.
FLOWERS Tubular, 5–6cm (2–2½in) long, and white. Produced from a lateral cephalium.
FLOWERING TIME Nocturnal, in summer.
ORIGIN Northern Peru.
CULTIVATION Grow in standard cactus compost, in full sun, at a minimum temperature of 10°C (50°F).

FEROCACTUS LATISPINUS

Broadly globular, bright lime-green cactus with a slightly flattened apex and prominent spination. The 15–23 ribs are divided by notches, producing a layered effect from top to bottom. The fruit is about 4cm (1½in) long and reddish.

SIZE 25–40cm (10–16in) in diameter.

AREOLES Large and grey-felted, set about 4cm (1½in) apart along the ribs.

SPINES 6–12 thin pale radials, about 2.5cm (1in) long. 4 thicker reddish centrals, up to 3.5cm (1½in) long, the lower one flattened and curving downwards with a hook at the tip.

FLOWERS Tubular, about 3.5cm (1½in) long, and whitish, reddish or purplish. Produced from the apex.

FLOWERING TIME Diurnal, in summer.

ORIGIN Central Mexico.

CULTIVATION Grow in standard cactus compost, in full sun, at a minimum temperature of 10°C (50°F). Popular and easily grown.

FEROCACTUS STAINESII

Prominently spined, globular cactus, becoming cylindrical and clustering. The stem has 15–20 ribs, each up to 4cm (1½in) tall.

SIZE 3m (10ft) tall, 60cm (2ft) in diameter.

AREOLES Set 3–4cm (1¼–1½in) apart along the ribs.

SPINES Reddish. 6–8 radials, up to 2cm (¾in) long. 4 curved centrals, up to 4cm (1½in) long.

FLOWERS Bell-shaped, 4cm (1½in) long, and orange-red. Produced from the apex.

FLOWERING TIME Diurnal, in midsummer.

ORIGIN Mexico (San Luis Potosi).

CULTIVATION Grow in standard cactus compost, in full sun, at a minimum temperature of 10°C (50°F).

FEROCACTUS VIRIDESCENS

Slightly elongated, globular cactus, often offsetting from the base. The glossy, deep green stem has 13–21 ribs and is prominently spined.
SIZE 45cm (18in) tall, 35cm (14in) in diameter.
AREOLES Short and whitish-woolly; set along the ribs.
SPINES Greenish-red. 9–20 radials, up to 2cm (¾in) long. 4 centrals, up to 4cm (1½in) long.
FLOWERS 3–4cm (1¼–1½in) long and yellowish-green. Produced from the apex.
FLOWERING TIME Diurnal, in summer.
ORIGIN Mexico (Baja).
CULTIVATION Grow in standard cactus compost, in full sun, at a minimum temperature of 10°C (50°F).

FRAILEA ASTEROIDES

Rather dwarf, globular cactus with a slightly concave apex. The reddish-brown stem has 10–15 slightly protruding ribs separated by heavy indentations.
SIZE 2.5cm (1in) in diameter.
AREOLES Small, and grey-felted; closely set in bead-like rows along the ribs.
SPINES 8 minute brown radials.
FLOWERS Open bell-shaped, about 3.5cm (1½in) in diameter, and creamy yellow. Produced in profusion from the centre of the apex, they offer an overall bloom area much larger than the plant itself.
FLOWERING TIME Diurnal, several appearing at once in summer.
ORIGIN Brazil, Uruguay.
CULTIVATION Grow in slightly porous, acid compost, in full sun, at a minimum temperature of 13°C (55°F).

GYMNOCACTUS
SUBTERRANEUS

Slightly elongated, globular cactus arising from a tuberous rootstock. The ribs of the bright green stems are divided into prominent tubercles.

SIZE 5cm (2in) tall, 3cm (1¼in) in diameter.

AREOLES White-woolly, with white bristles; set at the tips of the tubercles.

SPINES About 16 white radials, 6mm (¼in) long. 2 dark greyish centrals, about 2cm (¾in) long.

FLOWERS Funnel-shaped, 3cm (1¼in) across, and pinkish-violet. Produced from the apex.

FLOWERING TIME Diurnal, in summer.

ORIGIN Mexico (Tamaulipas).

CULTIVATION Grow in porous, slightly calcareous, enriched compost, in full sun, at a minimum temperature of 10°C (50°F).

GYMNOCALYCIUM
DENUDATUM

SPIDER CACTUS

Solitary, globular cactus with a concave centre to the apex. The dark grey green stem has 6–8 large, protruding, rounded ribs separated by deep indentations.

SIZE 7–15cm (3–6in) in diameter.

AREOLES Grey-felted; widely spaced with 2 sets of 3 per rib.

SPINES 4–8 whitish or greyish, 2cm (¾in) long, and prostrate on the surface of the stem.

FLOWERS Open-petalled and bell-shaped, about 5cm (2in) long and 7cm (3in) in diameter, with white petals and cream stamens. Produced from the apex.

FLOWERING TIME Diurnal, in midsummer.

ORIGIN Argentina, Brazil, Uruguay.

CULTIVATION Grow in standard cactus compost, in partial shade, at a minimum temperature of 10°C (50°F).

GYMNOCALYCIUM
MIHANOVICHII

PLAID CACTUS

Solitary, globular cactus with greyish- or reddish-green stems bearing usually 8 ribs, somewhat cross-banded.

SIZE 6cm (2½in) in diameter.

AREOLES Covered with a ball of white felt; set along the ribs at the junctions with the cross-banding.

SPINES 4–6 brownish radials, 1cm (½in) long.

FLOWERS Open-petalled, about 5cm (2in) in diameter, and bright pink. Produced at the end of a long tube that sprouts from near the apex.

FLOWERING TIME Diurnal, in early summer.

ORIGIN Paraguay (Bahia Negra).

CULTIVATION Grow in standard cactus compost, in partial shade, at a minimum temperature of 10°C (50°F).

GYMNOCALYCIUM
SPEGAZZINII

Solitary, globular cactus that is very popular in cultivation. The bluish- or greyish-green to brownish stem has 10–15 ribs.

SIZE 18cm (7in) in diameter.

AREOLES Yellowish-grey; set along the ribs.

SPINES Reddish-brown to greyish, 5–7 somewhat curved radials, up to 5.5cm (2in) long. Occasionally 1 central.

FLOWERS Funnel-shaped, 6–7cm (2½–3in) long, and white or pinkish-white with a reddish throat. Produced from around the apex.

FLOWERING TIME Diurnal, in midsummer.

ORIGIN Argentina (Salta).

CULTIVATION Grow in standard cactus compost, in slight shade, at a minimum temperature of 10°C (50°F).

HAAGEOCEREUS VERSICOLOR

Densely spiny, columnar cactus, a true desert species. The dark green stems are 5–6cm (2–2½in) in diameter and bear 16–22 ribs.
SIZE 1–2m (3–6ft) tall, 5–6cm (2–2½in) in diameter.
AREOLES Round and brown; set along the ribs.
SPINES Reddish, brown or yellowish. 20–30 radials, about 5mm (¼in) long. 1–2 centrals, up to 4cm (1½in) long.
FLOWERS About 8cm (3in) long and 6cm (2½in) across when fully open, white internally and green externally. Produced near the apex.
FLOWERING TIME Nocturnal, in summer.
ORIGIN Northern Peru.
CULTIVATION Grow in enriched mineral compost, in full sun, at a minimum temperature of 13°C (55°F).

HATIORA EPIPHYLLOIDES

A rare and choice, epiphytic cactus with more or less tubular, pendent stems. These are bright green and composed of joints up to 2.5cm (1in) long and 1cm (½in) in diameter.
SIZE Variable.
AREOLES Minute.
SPINES None.
FLOWERS About 1cm (½in) long, and yellowish.
FLOWERING TIME Diurnal, in spring.
ORIGIN Brazil (Rio de Janeiro, Sao Paulo).
CULTIVATION Grow in standard cactus compost, in partial shade, at a minimum temperature of 13°C (55°F). Difficult in cultivation and best grafted onto robust stock.

HILDEWINTERA AUREISPINA

Branching, spreading and trailing, columnar cactus with dense spines. The green stems, up to 1.5m (5ft) long and 2.5cm (1in) in diameter, have 16–17 ribs.

SIZE Variable.
AREOLES Set along the ribs.
SPINES 50 yellow, 0.4–1cm (⅛–½in) long.
FLOWERS Open-petalled, 4–6cm (1½–2½in) long and 5cm (2in) across, in various shades with a reddish central stripe to the narrow petals. Produced from the sides of the stems.
FLOWERING TIME Diurnal, in summer.
ORIGIN Bolivia.
CULTIVATION Grow in standard cactus compost, in full sun, at a minimum temperature of 10°C (50°F).

HOMALOCEPHALA TEXENSIS

HORSE CRIPPLER, DEVIL'S HEAD, CANDY CACTUS

Solitary, globular cactus whose slightly flattened apex has an irregularly shaped central area covered with dense cream felt. The greyish-green stem has 13–27 pronounced ribs and prominent spines. The fruit is round and red.

SIZE 10–15cm (4–6in) tall, 20–30cm (8–12in) in diameter.
AREOLES Large and cream-felt-covered; 2–7 per rib, set well apart.
SPINES 6–7 radials, up to 2cm (¾in) long, pinkish at first but taking on a yellowish tint with age. 1 thick central, similar but up to 6cm (2½in) or more long.
FLOWERS Bell-shaped, 5–6cm (2–2½in) long and across, with scales. Petals are pale reddish-pink with a satiny effect, fading from dark to lighter pink towards the centre. Outer petals have a spiny tip. Produced from the apex.
FLOWERING TIME Diurnal, in summer.
ORIGIN USA (New Mexico, Texas), northern Mexico.
CULTIVATION Grow in open, enriched mineral compost, in full sun, at a minimum temperature of 10°C (50°F).

HYLOCEREUS CALCARATUS

Tall, climbing semi-epiphytic cactus with elongated, 3-angled, bright green stems, 4–6cm (1½–2½in) wide. The margins of the ribs are divided into prominently rounded lobes.

SIZE Variable.

AREOLES Small, with one or more short white bristles; set immediately above one another on the lobes of the ribs.

SPINES None.

FLOWERS Cup-shaped, about 18cm (7in) across, with white or creamy white inner petals and greenish-white outer petals.

FLOWERING TIME Nocturnal, in mid-summer.

ORIGIN Costa Rica.

CULTIVATION Grow in rich, acid compost, in partial shade, at a minimum temperature of 15°C (59°F).

LEPISMIUM CRUCIFORME

Variable, pendent cactus with 3-angled stems, 30–60cm (12–24in) long and 2cm (¾in) wide. They are green with prominently notched reddish margins.

SIZE Variable.

AREOLES White; set 1 per notch along the edges of the stems.

SPINES None.

FLOWERS Solitary, 1–1.5cm (½in) long, and whitish. Produced in the notches.

FLOWERING TIME Diurnal, in spring.

ORIGIN Argentina, Brazil, Paraguay.

CULTIVATION Grow in standard cactus compost, in full shade, at a minimum temperature of 13°C (55°F).

LOBIVIA SILVESTRII

PEANUT CACTUS

Somewhat dwarf, columnar cactus, branching and offsetting freely. Each pale green stem has 7–10 low ribs.

SIZE 15cm (6in) long, 1–2.5cm (½–1in) in diameter.

AREOLES White- to cream-felt-covered; closely set along the ribs.

SPINES 10–15 bristly and whitish.

FLOWERS 5cm (2in) long and up to 10cm (4in) in diameter, and bright scarlet. Produced from scale- and hair-covered tubes on the apex.

FLOWERING TIME Diurnal, in summer.

ORIGIN Argentina (Tucuman).

CULTIVATION Grow in standard cactus compost, in partial shade, at a minimum temperature of 7°C (45°F). Will withstand lower temperatures if kept dry and in a bright location.

LOPHOCEREUS SCHOTTII

Erect or straggling, columnar cactus, branching from the base. The dull green stems, about 6cm (2¼in) thick, have 4–12 ribs and a terminal pseudocephalium.

SIZE 1–5m (3–15ft) tall.

AREOLES Large and woolly; set about 1cm (½in) apart along the ribs.

SPINES 4–7 blackish, 1cm (½in) long.

FLOWERS 3–4cm (1¼–1½in) long, red internally and green externally. Produced from the pseudocephalium.

FLOWERING TIME Nocturnal, in summer.

ORIGIN Mexico (Baja, Sonora).

CULTIVATION Grow in calcareous compost, in partial shade, at a minimum temperature of 10°C (50°F).

LOPHOPHORA WILLIAMSII

WHISKEY-BARREL CACTUS

Globular cactus with a flattened surface and concave apex filled with cream hair tufts. Many additional stems grow from the large taproot to form tightly spaced colonies. The bluish-green stems have 7–10 low ribs indistinctly divided into tubercles. The plant contains narcotic substances.

SIZE 5–8cm (2–3in) in diameter.

AREOLES Covered with cream hair tufts; set at the centre of each tubercle.

SPINES None.

FLOWERS Tubular, 1.2–1.5cm (½in) across, and pink or white. Produced from the centre of the apex.

FLOWERING TIME Diurnal, in summer.

ORIGIN Mexico (northern areas), USA (Texas).

CULTIVATION Grow in slightly calcareous compost, in full sun, at a minimum temperature of 7°C (45°F).

LOXANTHOCEREUS

GRANDITESSELLATUS

Sprawling cactus with a long, firm, cylindrical stem, about 5cm (2in) in diameter. This is bright green with 6–7 notched ribs. Likely to be reclassified within the genus *Cleistocactus*.

SIZE 2m (6ft) long.

AREOLES Round and white-woolly; set between the notches along the ribs.

SPINES Purplish-brown. 6–8 radials, up to 1cm (½in) long. 1 or rarely 2 centrals, up to 5cm (2in) long.

FLOWERS Somewhat tubular, 5–6cm (2–2½in) long, and red. Produced near the apex.

FLOWERING TIME Diurnal, in summer.

ORIGIN Central Peru.

CULTIVATION Grow in standard cactus compost, in full sun, at a minimum temperature of 13°C (55°F).

MAIHUENIOPSIS GLOMERATA

Thick, jointed, dull green cactus. Each joint is 2–3.5cm (¾–1½in) long.

SIZE 10cm (4in) tall.

AREOLES White with deeply set brown glochids; set on swellings of the stem.

SPINES 1–3 flat, about 3mm (⅛in) wide, produced from the upper areoles.

FLOWERS 3–3.5cm (1¼–1½in) across, and whitish.

FLOWERING TIME Diurnal, in summer.

ORIGIN Argentina.

CULTIVATION Grow in enriched mineral compost, in full sun, at a minimum temperature of 10°C (50°F).

MAMMILLARIA CHIONOCEPHALA

Solitary, finely spined, globular cactus that later develops offsets to form clusters. The bluish-green stems have 4-edged tubercles and thick white-woolly axils.

SIZE 12cm (5in) in diameter.

AREOLES Spiny at apex; variable lower down.

SPINES 22–24 white radials, up to 8mm (⅜in) long. 2–6 white or brownish centrals, up to 6mm (¼in) long, tipped with black and hooked.

FLOWERS White to pale pink with a reddish central stripe on the petals. Produced from the apex.

FLOWERING TIME Diurnal, in summer.

ORIGIN Mexico (Coahuila, Durango).

CULTIVATION Grow in standard cactus compost, in full sun, at a minimum temperature of 10°C (50°F).

Mammillaria Compressa

Globular to columnar cactus with a rounded, slightly concave apex. A variable species it readily offsets to form large clusters, each head about 8cm (3in) in diameter. The blue-green stems have prominent tubercles that are short, squat and imperfectly rounded with bristly, white-woolly axils. The oblong fruit is red.

SIZE 10cm (4in) tall, 20cm (8in) in diameter.
AREOLES White-felted in younger plants but naked in mature specimens; set on the tubercles.
SPINES 2–6 white or pale brownish radials, 2–7mm (¹⁄₁₆–¹⁄₄in) long.
FLOWERS Bell-shaped, up to 1.5cm (½in) long and across, and deep purplish-red.
FLOWERING TIME Diurnal, in summer.
ORIGIN Mexico (Queretaro, San Luis Potosi).
CULTIVATION Grow in standard cactus compost, in full sun, at a minimum temperature of 10°C (50°F).

Mammillaria Elongata

GOLDEN STAR CACTUS

Very variable, densely clustering cactus with both erect and prostrate, cylindrical stems, each 1–3cm (½–1¼in) thick and 6–15cm (2½–6in) long. The variously coloured spine formations provide very bright displays. The small, cone-shaped tubercles have yellowish felt at their bases.

SIZE Variable.
AREOLES Yellowish-felted.
SPINES 20 short radials, ranging from yellow to brown, often with differently coloured tips; they intertwine with spines of adjacent areoles to cover the entire surface of the stem. Up to 3 centrals, 9mm (³⁄₈in) long, although they are often absent.
FLOWERS Tubular, about 1.5cm (½in) long, and yellowish.
FLOWERING TIME Diurnal, in spring to summer.
ORIGIN Mexico (Hidalgo, Queretaro).
CULTIVATION Grow in standard cactus compost, in full sun, at a minimum temperature of 10°C (50°F).

MAMMILLARIA MICROCARPA

PINCUSHION CACTUS

Densely spined, columnar cactus, usually forming cushion-like clusters. The pale green stem has small, conical tubercles and bare axils.

SIZE 15cm (6in) tall, 3.5–4.4cm (1½–1¾in) in diameter.

AREOLES Set on the tubercles.

SPINES 18–30 whitish radials, up to 1.2cm (½in) long, and intertwining with spines from neighbouring areoles to cover the entire surface. 1–3 reddish-brown, almost black centrals, the bottom-most of which is hooked at the tip.

FLOWERS Bell-shaped, 2.5cm (1in) long and 2.8cm (1¼in) across, with bright pink petals. Produced around the apex.

FLOWERING TIME Diurnal, in summer.

ORIGIN Mexico (Chihuahua, Sonora), USA (Arizona).

CULTIVATION Grow in standard cactus compost containing a little lime, in full sun, at a minimum temperature of 10°C (50°F).

MATUCANA MADISONIORUM

Globular to slightly columnar cactus with a rounded, slightly concave apex. The grey-green to lime-green stem has 7–12 ribs, divided horizontally by deep furrows to give an almost tuberculate appearance. Older plants discharge black-brown seeds from globose fruits.

SIZE 10cm (4in) tall, 8cm (3in) in diameter.

AREOLES Grey-white felted, about 3mm (⅛in) wide; set at the apex of each tubercle with "veins" emanating from it.

SPINES 1 needle-like red-brown central, about 3cm (1¼in) long, in the area around the apex only.

FLOWERS Open-petalled, about 5cm (2in) in diameter, with pink-orange petals and yellow stamens. Produced at the end of a hairy tube, 10cm (4in) long, that grows from the centre of the apex.

FLOWERING TIME Diurnal, in mid-summer.

ORIGIN Peru (Amazonas).

CULTIVATION Grow in standard cactus compost, in partial shade, at a minimum temperature of 18°C (64°F).

MELOCACTUS MATANZANUS

Globular cactus with a pale yellowish-green stem bearing 8–10 heavily protruding ribs. More ribs often develop towards the top of the plant. The prominent cephalium, covered with burnt orange to reddish-brown bristles, is up to 9cm (3½in) high and 5–6cm (2–2½in) in diameter.

SIZE 9cm (3½in) in diameter.

AREOLES White-felted; set along the apical line of each rib.

SPINES Grey-white. 7 or 8 heavy, inwardly curving radials, 1–1.5cm (½in) long. 1 slightly longer central, up to 2cm (¾in) long.

FLOWERS Open-petalled, about 9cm (3½in) tall and 6cm (2½in) in diameter, and bright pink with yellow stamens. Produced from the cephalium.

FLOWERING TIME Diurnal (after mid-day), in summer.

ORIGIN Cuba.

CULTIVATION Grow in standard cactus compost, in full sun, at a minimum temperature of 16°C (61°F).

MITROCEREUS RUFICEPS

Tall, robust, tree-like, columnar cactus, branching from the main stem, which is about 40cm (16in) in diameter. Each stem has about 26 ribs.

SIZE 15m (50ft) tall.

AREOLES Set along the ribs.

SPINES 8–10 reddish radials, about 1cm (½in) long. 1–3 centrals, 4–5cm (1½–2in) long. All turn greyish with age.

FLOWERS Bell-shaped, about 5cm (2in) long, and pinkish-white. Produced from the top of the branches.

FLOWERING TIME Nocturnal, in summer.

ORIGIN Mexico (Puebla, Tehuacan).

CULTIVATION Grow in standard cactus compost, in full sun, at a minimum temperature of 13°C (55°F).

MONVILLEA CAMPINENSIS

Tall, slender, semi-erect, columnar cactus with bluish-green branches about 6cm (2½in) in diameter, each bearing 7–9 ribs.

SIZE 5m (15ft) tall.

AREOLES Grey-felted; set along the ribs.

SPINES 7–11 grey, up to 1.5cm (½in) long.

FLOWERS Flat-faced, about 10cm (4in) long and 6cm (2½in) across, and greenish-white. Produced from the tips of the branches.

FLOWERING TIME Nocturnal, in summer.

ORIGIN Brazil (Sao Paulo).

CULTIVATION Grow in standard cactus compost, in partial shade, at a minimum temperature of 10°C (50°F). Water freely in summer.

MYRTILLOCACTUS GEOMETRIZANS

Tree-like, columnar cactus, with a rounded apex, that develops many severely upward-curving branches. In cultivation it is much shorter and tends to branch from the base. The yellowish-green stems have 5 or 6 angular ribs separated by deep depressions which display sporadic areas of powdery blue. The fruit is round, about 7mm (¼in) in diameter, and pastel blue, sometimes blotched with green.

SIZE 4m (13ft) tall.

AREOLES Large and minimally grey-felted; set far apart along the ribs.

SPINES Brown radials, 4mm (⅛in) long. 1 flattened black central, 2.5–6cm (1–2¾in) long.

FLOWERS Tubular, about 3cm (1¼in) in diameter, with whitish to greenish petals. Produced from the upper areoles. Several may grow from one areole.

FLOWERING TIME Diurnal, in early summer.

ORIGIN Central Mexico to Guatemala.

CULTIVATION Grow in standard cactus compost, in full sun, at a minimum temperature of 10°C (50°F).

NEOBINGHAMIA
CLIMAXANTHA

Erect, columnar cactus with a bright green stem, 6–8cm (2½–3in) in diameter, bearing 19–27 ribs. There is a white-woolly pseudocephalium.

SIZE 1m (36in) tall.

AREOLES Brownish; set along the ribs.

SPINES 50–70 fine, bristly yellowish-brown radials, 5–8mm (¼–⅜in) long. 1–3 centrals, up to 2cm (¾in) long.

FLOWERS Tubular, 3–4cm (1¼–1½in) long, with white inner petals and rose-pink outer petals. Produced from the pseudocephalium.

FLOWERING TIME Nocturnal, in summer.

ORIGIN Peru (Eulalia).

CULTIVATION Grow in standard cactus compost, in full sun, at a minimum temperature of 13°C (55°F).

NEOBUXBAUMIA TETETZO

Tall, erect, columnar cactus of tree-like habit. The greyish-green stems, 30cm (1ft) in diameter, have 13–20 somewhat rounded ribs separated by deep furrows.

SIZE 15m (50ft) tall.

AREOLES Round and brownish; set at regular intervals along the ribs.

SPINES Blackish. 8–13 radials, up to 1.5cm (½in) long. 1 central, about 5cm (2in) long.

FLOWERS About 6cm (2½in) long, and whitish. Produced near the end of the apex.

FLOWERING TIME Nocturnal, in summer.

ORIGIN Mexico (Pueblo to Oaxaca).

CULTIVATION Grow in standard cactus compost, in full sun, at a minimum temperature of 13°C (55°F).

NEODAWSONIA APICICEPHALIUM

Impressive, tree-like, columnar cactus that offsets at the base to form small clusters. The bluish-green stems, 10cm (6in) in diameter, have 20–30 ribs. The small cephalium at the apex is covered with dense grey-white to creamy yellow wool.

SIZE 1–3m (3–10ft) tall.

AREOLES Elliptical and grey-white-felted; set along the ribs.

SPINES Fine, bristly and greyish-white. 9–12 radials, 2–3cm (¾–1¼in) long. 2–6 centrals, 2–4cm (¾–1½in) long.

FLOWERS Bell-shaped, 5–6cm (2–2½in) long and about 3cm (1¼in) across, with rose-pink petals suffused with yellow and an abundance of yellow stamens. Produced from the cephalium.

FLOWERING TIME Nocturnal, in summer.

ORIGIN Mexico (Oaxaca).

CULTIVATION Grow in standard cactus compost, in full sun, at a minimum temperature of 13°C (55°F).

NEOLLOYDIA CONOIDEA

Globular to cylindrical cactus with short, straight spines. The greyish-green stems bear oval tubercles with woolly axils.

SIZE 7–10cm (3–4in) tall, 7cm (3in) in diameter.

AREOLES Set at the tips of the tubercles.

SPINES White to greyish-black. 16 radials, up to 1cm (½in) long. 3–5 centrals, up to 3cm (1¼in) long.

FLOWERS About 6cm (2½in) across, and reddish-violet. Produced from the apex.

FLOWERING TIME Diurnal, in summer.

ORIGIN USA (Texas).

CULTIVATION Grow in porous, enriched mineral compost, in full sun, at a minimum temperature of 10°C (50°F).

NEOPORTERIA SETIFLORA

Globular cactus with short straight spines. The bluish-green stem has about 15 ribs.

SIZE Up to 1.5m (5ft) tall.

AREOLES Large and brownish-white-felted; set along the ribs.

SPINES 8–10 reddish-grey radials. About 4 centrals, up to 2.5cm (1in) long.

FLOWERS Open-petalled, 3cm (1¼in) long, and pale yellow, often with orange shading. Produced from the apex.

FLOWERING TIME Diurnal, in late summer.

ORIGIN Argentina (Mendoza).

CULTIVATION Grow in standard cactus compost, in partial shade, at a minimum temperature of 10°C (50°F).

NEORAIMONDIA ROSEIFLORA

Bushy, columnar cactus with a thick greyish-green stem bearing 5 ribs. These have prominent warts.

SIZE 2m (6ft) tall.

AREOLES Large and consisting of tufts of brownish bristles; set on the tips of the warts.

SPINES Greyish-white, 10cm (4in) or more long.

FLOWERS Tubular, 4–5cm (1½–2in) long, including the brown-felted tube. Pinkish-red petals have a purplish central stripe and there is an abundance of protruding stamens. Produced from near the apex.

FLOWERING TIME Diurnal, in summer.

ORIGIN Peru (Chosica).

CULTIVATION Grow in standard cactus compost, in full sun, at a minimum temperature of 13°C (59°F).

NEOWERDERMANNIA VORWERKII

Globular cactus with a dark greyish-green stem bearing 16 or more tuberculate ribs.

SIZE 6–8cm (2½–3in) in diameter.

AREOLES Grey-white-felted; set in depressions between the tubercles.

SPINES 10 brownish radials, up to 1.5cm (½in) long. 1 central, often hooked.

FLOWERS Open-petalled, 2–2.5cm (¾–1in) long and across, and white or pale lilac-pink. Produced at the apex.

FLOWERING TIME Diurnal, in summer.

ORIGIN Northern Argentina, northern Bolivia.

CULTIVATION Grow in enriched mineral compost, in full sun, at a minimum temperature of 7°C (45°F). Keep dry in winter.

NOPALXOCHIA PHYLLANTHOIDES

Slender, branching, epiphytic cactus. The soft, strap-like branches, 30–45cm (12–18in) long, are bright green in colour with scalloped margins.

SIZE Variable.

AREOLES Very small and brownish; set along the margins of the branches.

SPINES None.

FLOWERS 7–9cm (3–3½in) long, on a tube about 2cm (¾in) long, and various shades of pink. Produced from the margins of the branches.

FLOWERING TIME Diurnal, in late spring to early summer.

ORIGIN Mexico (Puebla).

CULTIVATION Grow in standard cactus compost, in filtered light, at a minimum temperature of 10°C (50°F). Water with care.

NOTOCACTUS POLYACANTHUS

Woolly-crowned, globular cactus producing numerous offsets. The dark green stems have 17 notched ribs.

SIZE 10cm (4in) in diameter.

AREOLES White; set about 1cm (½in) apart along the ribs.

SPINES 6–8 whitish radials, up to 1cm (½in). Usually 1 longer central.

FLOWERS 1.5–2cm (½–¾in) diameter and canary yellow with prominent reddish stigma lobes. Produced in clusters on the apex.

FLOWERING TIME Diurnal, in early summer.

ORIGIN Southern Brazil.

CULTIVATION Grow in standard cactus compost, in full sun, at a minimum temperature of 10°C (50°F).

OBREGONIA DENEGREI

STARBURST CACTUS

Globular cactus with a thick taproot. The centre of the apex is covered with white felt. The stem is covered with flat, leaf-like, greyish or brownish green tubercles which are spirally arranged and about 1.5cm (½in) long and 2.5cm (1in) wide at the base.

SIZE 8–12cm (3–5in) in diameter.

AREOLES Small, round and white-felted; set at the tips of the tubercles.

SPINES 4 heavily curved and greenish, falling off as the plant matures.

FLOWERS Open-petalled, 2–4cm (1–1½in) in diameter, and white or pinkish with a scaly appearance. Produced from the centre of the apex.

FLOWERING TIME Diurnal, in summer.

ORIGIN Mexico (Tamaulipas).

CULTIVATION Grow in standard cactus compost, in full sun, at a minimum temperature of 10°C (50°F).

OPUNTIA BASILARIS

Bushy cactus with almost oval, bluish- or reddish-green joints, 10–20cm (4–8in) long, with a velvety appearance.
SIZE Variable.
AREOLES Brownish with reddish-brown bristles; set over the surface of each joint.
SPINES Sometimes 1 short spine.
FLOWERS Open-petalled, 6–8cm (2½–3in) long and across, annd reddish-purple. Produced from the edges of the joints.
FLOWERING TIME Diurnal, in early summer.
ORIGIN Northern Mexico, USA (Arizona, Nevada).
CULTIVATION Grow in porous, enriched mineral compost, in full sun, at a minimum temperature of 7°C (45°F).

OPUNTIA ERECTOCLADA

Sometimes prostrate, columnar cactus, offsetting to form dense clumps. The dark green joints, about 5cm (2in) long and 4cm (1½in) wide, are narrowly oblong and flat.
SIZE Variable.
AREOLES With reddish-brown bristles; set along the apex of each stem angle.
SPINES 2–4 red-brown radials, 1cm (½in) long.
FLOWERS Open-petalled, about 4cm (1½in) in diameter, and bright orange-red. Produced from the apex.
FLOWERING TIME Diurnal, in summer.
ORIGIN Argentina.
CULTIVATION Grow in standard cactus compost, in partial shade, at a minimum temperature of 10°C (50°F).

OPUNTIA FALCATA

Tree-like cactus with glossy, dark green joints up to 35cm (14in) long and 9cm (3½in) wide. The flattened surfaces are marked with somewhat obscure prominences.

SIZE 1.5m (5ft) tall.

AREOLES Whitish; set on the surface of the joints.

SPINES 2–8 long, needle-like, rough and pale brownish or yellowish, 1cm (½in) or more long.

FLOWERS Open-petalled, 3–5cm (1¼–2in) across, and reddish. Produced from the edges of the joints.

FLOWERING TIME Diurnal, in summer.

ORIGIN Haiti.

CULTIVATION Grow in standard cactus compost, in partial shade, at a minimum temperature of 13°C (55°F).

OREOCEREUS CELSIANUS

OLD MAN OF THE MOUNTAINS CACTUS

Erect, columnar cactus, with a rounded apex, branching from the base to form small groups. The bright blue-green stems, 2m (6ft) tall and 8–12cm (3–5in) in diameter, have 10–18 rounded ribs that protrude where the areoles appear.

SIZE Variable.

AREOLES Large and white-woolly, with tufts of silky hairs; set about 1.5cm (½in) apart along the ribs.

SPINES 9 heavy, cone-shaped brown radials, 2cm (¾in) long. Up to 4 heavier red-brown centrals, up to 7cm (3in) long.

FLOWERS Tubular, 7–9cm (3–3½in) long, with dark pink petals; borne on a hairy tube. Produced near the apex.

FLOWERING TIME Diurnal, in summer.

ORIGIN Argentina, Bolivia.

CULTIVATION Grow in standard cactus compost, in full sun, at a minimum temperature of 10°C (50°F).

OROYA PERUVIANA

Flattened, globular cactus with a bluish-green stem bearing 12–13 rounded ribs that are notched into long tubercles.

SIZE 10cm (4in) tall, 15cm (6in) in diameter.

AREOLES Linear and nearly 1cm (½in) long; set on the tubercles.

SPINES Yellowish-brown. Radials, about 1cm (½in) long, are arranged in a comb-like fashion. To 6 centrals, up to 3cm (1¼in) long.

FLOWERS Bell-shaped, about 2.5cm (1in) long, with pale pink petals, yellowish at the base and reddish externally. Produced from new areoles on the apex.

FLOWERING TIME Diurnal, in summer.

ORIGIN Central Peru.

CULTIVATION Grow in standard cactus compost, in full sun, at a minimum temperature of 13°C (55°F).

PACHYCEREUS
WEBERI

Giant, tree-like, columnar cactus branching from well above the base and often found in small groups. The erect, almost bluish-green branches are 10cm (4in) or more thick and have 8–10 protruding ribs.

SIZE 3m (10ft) tall.

AREOLES Elongated and brown-felted; set about 3–5cm (1¼–2in) apart along the ribs.

SPINES Grey to black. 7–9 radials, 1cm (½in) long. 1 flat central, up to 10cm (4in) long.

FLOWERS Tubular, up to 10cm (4in) long, and pink. Produced from the apex.

FLOWERING TIME Nocturnal, in midsummer.

ORIGIN Mexico (Oaxaca, Puebla).

CULTIVATION Grow in standard cactus compost, in full sun, at a minimum temperature of 13°C (55°F).

PARODIA CLAVICEPS

Club-shaped, more or less cylindrical cactus with a dark green stem bearing about 26 ribs.

SIZE 50cm (20in) tall, 12cm (5in) in diameter.

AREOLES Whitish; set along the ribs.

SPINES Drooping, soft and yellowish, up to 1cm (½in) long.

FLOWERS Open-petalled, 4–5cm (1½–2in) across, and sulphur-yellow. Produced singly from the centre of the apex.

FLOWERING TIME Diurnal, in midsummer.

ORIGIN Brazil, Paraguay.

CULTIVATION Grow in standard cactus compost, in full sun, at a minimum temperature of 10°C (50°F).

PARODIA MUTABILIS

Globular, glaucous-green cactus with a white-woolly crown and spirally arranged ribs.

SIZE 8cm (3in) in diameter.

AREOLES White-woolly; set along the ribs.

SPINES 50 whitish radials. Most usually 4 centrals, up to about 1.2cm (½in) long.

FLOWERS Funnel-shaped, 3–5cm (1¼–2in) across when fully open, and bright golden yellow. Produced in clusters from the apex.

FLOWERING TIME Diurnal, in summer.

ORIGIN Argentina (Salta). At high altitudes.

CULTIVATION Grow in standard cactus compost, in full sun, at a minimum temperature of 10°C (50°F).

PEDIOCACTUS SILERI

Somewhat egg-shaped cactus with 12–14 spirally arranged ribs notched into tubercles.

SIZE 15cm (6in) tall, 12cm (5in) in diameter.

AREOLES Prominent and circular; set at the tips of the tubercles.

SPINES Short and straight. 11–15 white radials up to 2cm (¾in) long. 3–7 brownish-black centrals, about 3cm (1¼in) long, becoming almost white with age.

FLOWERS Open-petalled, 2.5cm (1in) or more in diameter, and yellowish. Produced from the apex.

FLOWERING TIME Diurnal, in summer.

ORIGIN USA (northern Arizona, Utah). At high altitudes.

CULTIVATION Grow in porous, humus-enriched mineral compost, in full sun, at a minimum temperature of 7°C (45°F).

PELECYPHORA ASELLIFORMIS

Small, somewhat globular cactus which has stems covered with flat, laterally compressed greyish-green tubercles that are spirally arranged. The pattern of areoles resembles white fossilized ferns.

SIZE 5–10cm (2–4in) tall, 2–5cm (¾–2in) in diameter.

AREOLES Long and narrow; set at the tips of the tubercles. Additional cream-coloured wool covers much of the space between them.

SPINES Numerous and minute, arranged in a comb-like formation.

FLOWERS Bell-shaped, about 3–4cm (1¼–1½in) in diameter, with white outer petals and reddish-purple inner petals. Produced from the apex.

FLOWERING TIME Diurnal, in summer.

ORIGIN Mexico (San Luis Potosi).

CULTIVATION Grow in permeable, enriched mineral compost, in full sun, at a minimum temperature of 13°C (55°F).

PERESKIA ACULEATA

Climbing, trailing cactus with stems 8–10m (25–30ft) long and 1cm (½in) thick, bearing dark green leaves up to 9cm (3½in) long and 4cm (1½in) wide.
SIZE Variable.
AREOLES No bristles.
SPINES 1–3.
FLOWERS Rose-like, up to 4.5cm (1¾in) across, with whitish-yellow petals shading to pinkish at the base and pink stamens. Produced along the stems.
FLOWERING TIME Diurnal, in late summer.
ORIGIN Brazil, Paraguay, USA (Florida), West Indies.
CULTIVATION Grow in standard cactus compost, in full sun, at a minimum temperature of 10°C (50°F).

PFEIFFERA IANTHOTHELE

Epiphytic on forest trees, this pendent cactus has bright green stems, 30–50cm (12–20in) long and 1.5cm (½in) wide, and usually 4-angled. Flowers are followed by pinkish fruits.
SIZE Variable.
AREOLES Set along the ribs.
SPINES 6 / yellowish, about 5mm (¼in) long.
FLOWERS Bell-shaped, 2.5cm (1in) long, with yellow inner petals and pinkish-purple outer petals. Produced along the ribs.
FLOWERING TIME Diurnal, in early summer.
ORIGIN Argentina, Bolivia.
CULTIVATION Grow in standard cactus compost, in partial shade, at a minimum temperature of 10°C (50°F).

PILOSOCEREUS PURPUSII

WOOLLY TORCH CACTUS

Columnar, sometimes prostrate cactus branching from the base. The bright green stems, 3m (10ft) long and 3–4cm (1¼–1½in) in diameter, have 12 ribs. There is a white-hairy cephalium at the apex.
SIZE Variable.
AREOLES White-felted and sporting long, wispy hairs; closely set in rows along the ribs.
SPINES Generally yellowish becoming grey with age. Varying in number and up to 3cm (1¼in) long.
FLOWERS Open funnel-shaped, about 7cm (3in) long and across, and pale pinkish-rose with white edges. Produced from the cephalium.
FLOWERING TIME Nocturnal, in midsummer.
ORIGIN Mexico (Sinaloa, Sonora).
CULTIVATION Grow in standard cactus compost, in full sun, at a minimum temperature of 10°C (50°F).

POLASKIA CHICHIPE

Slender, tree-like, columnar cactus, heavily branching from basal offsets. The pale green stems are 5–7cm (2–3in) thick with 7–12 acute ribs, each 2cm (¾in) deep with swellings.
SIZE 4–5m (12–15ft) tall.
AREOLES Grey-felted; set about 1.5cm (½in) apart on the swellings.
SPINES Blackish-brown fading to greyish. 6–7 radials, up to 1cm (½in) long. 1 central, about 1.5cm (½in) long.
FLOWERS Widely open-petalled, about 3cm (1¼in) long and 4cm (1½in) in diameter, with creamy white to greenish-yellow petals, each with a reddish central stripe and protruding stamens. Produced from the sides of apex.
FLOWERING TIME Diurnal, in summer.
ORIGIN Mexico (Oaxaca, Puebla).
CULTIVATION Grow in standard cactus compost, in full sun, at a minimum temperature of 13°C (55°F).

PTEROCACTUS RETICULATUS

A clump-forming cactus that grows from a tuberous rootstock with tubers about 20cm (8in) long and 10cm (4in) in diameter. The cylindrical, jointed stems are 1–2cm (½–¾in) in diameter, reddish-grey and with many, very shallow "warts" below each areole.

SIZE 2–3cm (¾–1¼in) long (stems).
AREOLES Set in spiralling rows on the surface of each joint.
SPINES 1–3 minute and whitish.
FLOWERS Open-petalled, about 4cm (1½in) across, and yellow. Produced from the apex.
FLOWERING TIME Diurnal, in early summer.
ORIGIN Argentina (San Juan).
CULTIVATION Grow in standard cactus compost, in full sun, at a minimum temperature of 10°C (50°F).

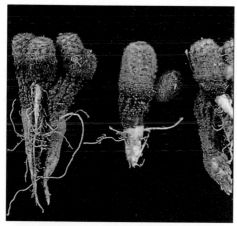

PYGMAEOCEREUS BYLESIANUS

Semi-columnar to globular cactus growing from a long, fleshy taproot. The dark green stem has 12–14 ribs.

SIZE 10cm (4in) tall.
AREOLES Round; set along the ribs.
SPINES Fine, greyish radials. 1 or 2 longer centrals, up to 3–5mm (⅛–¼in) long.
FLOWERS 6cm (2½in) long, with white inner petals and pale greenish outer petals. Produced from a tube on the apex.
FLOWERING TIME Nocturnal, in midsummer.
ORIGIN Southern Peru.
CULTIVATION Grow in very porous, enriched mineral compost, in full sun, at a minimum temperature of 10°C (50°F). Be careful not to damage the taproot.

QUIABENTIA ZEHTNERI

Tall, bushy cactus with slender, cylindrical stems and roundish or oval-shaped leaves, 2–4cm (¾–1½in) long.

SIZE 2–3m (6–10ft) tall.

AREOLES White-felted; set along the stems.

SPINES Numerous, short, fine and whitish.

FLOWERS Funnel-shaped, about 4cm (1½in) long, opening to 8cm (3in) in diameter, and reddish-pink.

FLOWERING TIME Diurnal, in summer.

ORIGIN Brazil (Bahia).

CULTIVATION Grow in enriched mineral compost, in full sun, at a minimum temperature of 13°C (55°F). Water carefully at all times.

REBUTIA HELIOSA

Slightly flattened, globular to semi-columnar cactus that offsets freely to form cushion-like clusters. The small greyish-green stem has 35–40 ribs, arranged spirally, with small tubercles.

SIZE 2cm (¾in) tall, 1.5–2.5cm (½–1in) in diameter.

AREOLES Brown-felted; set along the ribs.

SPINES 24–26 comb-like radials. No centrals.

FLOWERS Trumpet-shaped, 4.5–5.5cm (1¾–2in) long and 4cm (1½in) in diameter, and orange or reddish.

FLOWERING TIME Diurnal, in summer.

ORIGIN Bolivia (Tarija).

CULTIVATION Grow in standard cactus compost, in partial shade, at a minimum temperature of 10°C (50°F).

REBUTIA SENILIS

Flattened to globular cactus that clusters freely. The deep green stems have 18 spirally arranged ribs divided into tubercles. On rare occasions, an interesting cristate form develops usually with the spiralling arrangement much in evidence and a profusion of flowers.

SIZE 8cm (3in) tall, 7cm (3in) in diameter.

AREOLES White; set along the ribs.

SPINES 25 fine and yellowish-white, about 3cm (1¼in) long and often matted together.

FLOWERS Open-petalled, 3.5cm (1½in) in diameter, and carmine red. Produced in clusters around the apex.

FLOWERING TIME Diurnal, in summer.

ORIGIN Argentina.

CULTIVATION Grow in standard cactus compost, in full sun, at a minimum temperature of 10°C (50°F).

RHIPSALIDOPSIS ROSEA

Small, shrubby cactus with erect or pendent stems composed of flat, sometimes angular segments, 2–4cm (¾–1¾in) long and up to 1cm (½in) wide. These usually have fine reddish margins. The terminal segment has scalloped edges.

SIZE Variable.

AREOLES Minute, with a few bristly hairs; set along the edges of the terminal segments, with a single, larger areole at the tip.

SPINES None.

FLOWERS Pond-lily-like, about 3–4cm (1¼–1½in) in diameter and bright powdery pink. As many as 3 may be produced from the longer areole on the terminal segment, but only once.

FLOWERING TIME Diurnal, in spring and early summer.

ORIGIN Brazil (forests of Parana).

CULTIVATION Grow in porous, enriched mineral compost, in partial shade, at a minimum temperature of 10°C (50°F).

RHIPSALIS RUSSELLII

Densely clustering cactus from forested regions, epiphytic on trees. The broad, leaf-like segments, 15cm (6in) long and 5–6cm (2–2½in) wide, have scalloped margins edged with reddish-purple and are particularly prominently veined. The fruit is purple.

SIZE Variable.

AREOLES Whitish; set along the scalloped edges of the joints.

SPINES None.

FLOWERS About 3mm (⅛in) long, and whitish. Produced singly or in clusters from the areoles.

FLOWERING TIME Diurnal, in early summer.

ORIGIN Brazil (Bahia).

CULTIVATION Grow in standard cactus compost, in partial shade, at a minimum temperature of 10°C (50°F).

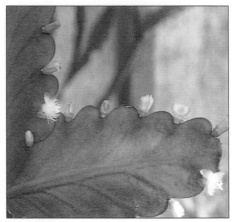

SCHLUMBERGERA OPUNTIOIDES

Branching, pendent cactus, heavily divided into flattened segments. These are thick, fleshy and deep green, about 2.5–6cm (1–2½in) long and 1–2cm (½–¾in) wide.

SIZE Variable.

AREOLES White-felted; set in rows across the surface of the segments.

SPINES Widely varying number of tiny off-white radials.

FLOWERS Tubular with backward-curving petals, about 4.5cm (1¾in) long, and red with areas of white. Produced from the terminal segments.

FLOWERING TIME Diurnal, in late spring.

ORIGIN Brazil (Minas Gerais).

CULTIVATION Grow in standard cactus compost, in partial shade, at a minimum temperature of 13°C (55°F).

SCLEROCACTUS PAPYRACANTHUS

Short, globular to cylindrical cactus, occurring as a solitary plant or in groups. The stem has 8–13 ribs with prominent tubercles.

SIZE 8cm (3in) tall, 3.5cm (1½in) in diameter.
AREOLES Set at the tips of the tubercles.
SPINES 5–9 whitish radials, 3–4mm (⅛in) long. 3–4 flat, curving centrals, 1–2cm (½–¾in) long and often intertwining.
FLOWERS About 2cm (¾in) long, and whitish. Produced from the centre of the apex.
FLOWERING TIME Diurnal, in summer.
ORIGIN USA (Arizona, New Mexico).
CULTIVATION Grow in standard cactus compost containing a little lime, in full sun, at a minimum temperature of 10°C (50°F). Water very carefully.

SELENICEREUS GRANDIFLORUS

Variable, climbing or trailing cactus, epiphytic on forest trees. The slender stems, 5m (15ft) long and 2–3cm (¾–1¼in) thick, have 5–8 ribs. The fruit is spiny and plum-like.

SIZE Variable.
AREOLES Pale and yellowish-woolly; set along the ribs.
SPINES 7–11 yellow, ageing to grey.
FLOWERS Fragrant and peony-like, about 30cm (12in) long and 15cm (6in) across, with broad white petals and narrow, pale yellowish-brown sepals. Produced near the stem tips.
FLOWERING TIME Nocturnal, in summer.
ORIGIN Mexico, West Indies.
CULTIVATION Grow in porous, enriched mineral compost, in partial shade, at a minimum temperature of 15°C (59°F).

STENOCEREUS GUMMOSUS

Bushy, columnar cactus, branching from the base. The greyish-green stems are 4–6cm (1½–2½in) thick and have 8–9 ribs.
SIZE 1m (36in) tall.
AREOLES Set 2cm (¾in) apart along the ribs.
SPINES 8–12 radials, up to 1cm (½in) long. 4–6 centrals, 4cm (1½in) long.
FLOWERS 10–14cm (4–5½in) long, and purplish-red. Produced on a slender tube.
FLOWERING TIME Nocturnal, in early summer.
ORIGIN Mexico (Bahia).
CULTIVATION Grow in porous, enriched calcareous compost, in full sun, at a minimum temperature of 13°C (55°F).

STROMBOCACTUS DISCIFORMIS

Globular cactus, very rarely offsetting. The apex is slightly flattened with a few persistent white spines at the centre. The grey-brown stem has 12–18 ribs formed into flat, closely set, diamond-shaped tubercles that are raised in the centres. The cristate form, which gives 2 crowns, is rarely encountered.
SIZE 5–12cm (2–5in) in diameter.
AREOLES White-felted; set at the tips of the tubercles.
SPINES 1–5 greyish-white, 1.5cm (½in) long.
FLOWERS Open funnel-shaped, about 4cm (1½in) across and slightly less than 4cm (1½in) long, and white or yellowish. Produced from the apex.
FLOWERING TIME Diurnal, in summer.
ORIGIN Mexico (Hidalgo).
CULTIVATION Grow in enriched mineral compost, in full sun, at a minimum temperature of 10°C (50°F). Water with care and keep dry in winter.

SUBPILOCEREUS REPANDUS

Tall, columnar cactus, often tree-like in its habitat. The many greyish- to bluish-green branches, up to 10cm (4in) in diameter, bear 8–12 ribs about 1cm (½in) high.

SIZE 10m (30ft) tall.

AREOLES Greyish-white; set along the ribs.

SPINES Numerous, fine, bristle-like and whitish, with one or more centrals, up to 5cm (2in) long.

FLOWERS Funnel-shaped, 10cm (4in) long and 4cm (1½in) in diameter, with white inner petals and greenish-white or pale pinkish outer segments.

FLOWERING TIME Nocturnal, in summer.

ORIGIN Curacao.

CULTIVATION Grow in standard cactus compost, in full sun, at a minimum temperature of 18°C (64°F).

SULCOREBUTIA RAUSCHII

Globular cactus with a slightly concave apex, offsetting at the base to form sparse clusters. The small blackish- or purplish-green stems have up to 16 ribs divided into 6-sided tubercles.

SIZE 2cm (¾in) tall, 3cm (1¼in) in diameter (stem).

AREOLES Naked and about 2mm (¹⁄₁₆in) long; set at the centre of the tubercles.

SPINES 11–12 thin yellowish radials, 1mm (¹⁄₁₆in) long. Rarely, up to 2 slightly longer centrals.

FLOWERS Open-petalled, about 3cm (1¼in) long and across, with bright pink petals and creamy yellow stamens. Produced from the side of the stem.

FLOWERING TIME Diurnal, in early to midsummer.

ORIGIN Bolivia (Chuquisaca).

CULTIVATION Grow in standard cactus compost, in full sun, at a minimum temperature of 10°C (50°F).

73

TEPHROCACTUS GEOMETRICUS

Jointed cactus with almost spherical greyish-green joints up to 3.5cm (1½in) in diameter.

SIZE 15cm (6in) tall.

AREOLES Brownish, with minute bristles; set regularly over the surface of the joints.

SPINES 3–5 whitish or brownish, 0.5–1cm (¼–½in) long, and soon falling.

FLOWERS About 3cm (1¼in) long, and white.

FLOWERING TIME Diurnal, in midsummer.

ORIGIN Argentina (Catamarca).

CULTIVATION Grow in standard cactus compost, in full sun, at a minimum temperature of 10°C (50°F).

THELOCACTUS RINCONENSIS

Mostly solitary, globular cactus with a flattened or concave apex containing white wool. The greyish- or bluish-green stem has usually 13 ribs divided into very prominent, angled tubercles, each up to 1cm (½in) high.

SIZE 6–8cm (2½–3in) tall, 12cm (5in) in diameter.

AREOLES Set at the tips of the tubercles.

SPINES 3–4 greyish-brown or black, up to 1.5cm (½in) long.

FLOWERS Open funnel-shaped, about 4cm (1½in) in diameter, and white with a pinkish central stripe on each petal. Produced from the apex.

FLOWERING TIME Diurnal, in early summer.

ORIGIN Mexico (Coahuila).

CULTIVATION Grow in calcareous compost, in full sun, at a minimum temperature of 13°C (55°F).

TRICHOCEREUS HUASCHA

Slender, sprawling or trailing cactus, offsetting freely from the base. The dark green stems, 50–90cm (20–36in) tall and 5–8cm (2–3in) in diameter, are strongly spined and have 12–18 ribs.
SIZE Variable.
AREOLES Whitish-brown; very closely set along the ribs.
SPINES 9–11 brownish radials, up to 4cm (1½in) long, 1–2 centrals, up to 6cm (2½in) long.
FLOWERS Solitary, tubular, 7–10cm (3–4in) long, and golden yellow or red. Produced from the sides of the apex.
FLOWERING TIME Diurnal, in midsummer.
ORIGIN Argentina.
CULTIVATION Grow in standard cactus compost, in full sun, at a minimum temperature of 10°C (50°F).

TURBINICARPUS PSEUDOMACROCHELE

Miniature, globular cactus offsetting from around the apex to produce heads 3–4cm (1¼–1½in) across. The dull green stems have ribs divided into small tubercles.
SIZE Variable.
AREOLES White; set at the tips of the tubercles.
SPINES 6–8 adpressed, borne on terminal areoles.
FLOWERS Open-petalled, about 3.5cm (1½in) in diameter, and pale pinkish with a pale reddish central stripe on each petal. Produced near the apex.
FLOWERING TIME Diurnal, in summer.
ORIGIN Mexico (San Luis Potosi).
CULTIVATION Grow in enriched mineral compost, in full sun, at a minimum temperature of 10°C (50°F).

U E B E L M A N N I A
P E C T I N I F E R A

Distinctive and attractive, globular to slightly columnar cactus. The reddish, almost blackish-brown stem has 15–18 prominent ribs with outwardly projecting spines that produce an interesting, comb-like effect.

SIZE 50cm (20in) tall, 10–15cm (4–6in) in diameter.

AREOLES Brown-felted; closely set in single rows along the apex of the ribs.

SPINES No radials. Straight, dark brownish centrals, up to 1.5cm (½in) long.

FLOWERS Open-petalled, about 1.5cm (½in) long and 1cm (½in) across, and lemon-yellow. Produced from the apex.

FLOWERING TIME Diurnal, in summer.

ORIGIN Brazil (Minas Gerais).

CULTIVATION Grow in permeable, enriched, slightly calcareous compost, in full sun, at a minimum temperature of 15°C (59°F). A humid atmosphere is required.

W E B E R O C E R E U S G L A B E R

Sprawling or trailing, epiphytic cactus, climbing by means of aerial roots. The glaucous-green stems, 2–3m (6–10ft) long and 2cm (¾in) thick, are 3-angled and more or less toothed.

SIZE Variable.

AREOLES Small and brownish-woolly; set along the angles of the stem.

SPINES 1–2 very short spines.

FLOWERS Cup-shaped, 10–12cm (4–5in) across, with serrate-edged white inner petals and pale greenish-brown outer petals. Produced towards the stem tips.

FLOWERING TIME Nocturnal, in midsummer.

ORIGIN Guatemala.

CULTIVATION Grow in standard cactus compost, in partial shade, at a minimum temperature of 15°C (59°F).

WEINGARTIA NEOCUMMINGII

Variable, semi-globular cactus with a bright to dark green stem bearing 16–18 tuberculate ribs.

SIZE 20cm (8in) tall, 10cm (4in) in diameter.

AREOLES Set at the tips of the tubercles.

SPINES 16–20 brown-tipped yellowish radials, up to 1.5cm (½in) long. About 6 more, thick centrals.

FLOWERS 2.5cm (1in) long, and orange shading to a yellow throat. Produced from the apex.

FLOWERING TIME Diurnal, in summer.

ORIGIN Bolivia.

CULTIVATION Grow in standard cactus compost, in full sun, at a minimum temperature of 10°C (50°F).

WILCOXIA POSELGERI

Fairly rigid, erect and bushy, columnar cactus. The branching, cylindrical, dark green stems, 60cm (24in) tall and 1.5cm (½in) or more in diameter, have 8–10 shallow ribs.

SIZE Variable.

AREOLES Off-white-felted; closely set along the ribs.

SPINES Greyish-white. 8–9 radials, up to 2mm (¹⁄₁₆in) long. 1 or 2 centrals, 8mm (³⁄₈in) or so long.

FLOWERS Open-petalled, 4–5cm (1½–2in) long and across, and pale purplish-pink with a reddish throat. Produced near the stem tips.

FLOWERING TIME Diurnal, in summer (after mid-day).

ORIGIN Mexico (Coahuila), USA (Texas).

CULTIVATION Grow in standard cactus compost, in indirect sunlight, at a minimum temperature of 10°C (50°F).

WILMATTEA MINUTIFLORA

Sprawling or trailing, epiphytic cactus, climbing on trees by means of aerial roots. The elongated, 3-angled, dark green stems have joints 1.5–2.5cm (½–1in) wide with evenly scalloped margins.
SIZE Variable.
AREOLES Set about 3cm (1¼in) apart along the angles of the stem.
SPINES 1–3 minute, almost hair-like and yellowish to black, about 1mm (¹⁄₁₆in) long.
FLOWERS Fragrant, 3–3.5cm (1¼–1½in) long and 8–9cm (3–3½in) wide when open fully, white on the inside and red externally. When the flower is closed, the short tube and small ovary, which are covered with triangular green scales and edged at the tips with brownish-red, can be seen. Produced from the sides of the stem.
FLOWERING TIME Nocturnal, in early summer.
ORIGIN Guatemala, Honduras.
CULTIVATION Grown in standard cactus compost, in partial shade, at a minimum temperature of 13°C (55°F).

PICTURE CREDITS

The authors and publishers have made every effort to identify the copyright owners of the pictures used in this book; they apologize for any omissions and would like to thank the following:
Dr W. Barthlott; Pierre Braun; John Donald; Charles Glass; Robert Holt; Clive Innes; Robert Foster; Kenneth Heil; Myron Kimnach; B. E. Leuenberger; A. J. S. McMillan; Dr W. Rauh; Tegelberg Nurseries; V. Turecek.

GLOSSARY

AREOLE: cushion-like growing point of a cactus.

BRISTLE: stiffened hair.

CALCAREOUS: of or containing lime or chalk.

CALLUS: hardened plant tissue forming over a cut or wound.

CENTRAL SPINES: spines arising from the centre of the areole.

CEPHALIUM: densely woolly, bristly "head" formed on certain cacti, from which flowers are produced.

DIURNAL: day-flowering.

ERECT: upright.

FAMILY: taxonomic grouping of similar genera.

GENUS: taxonomic grouping of species with similar characteristics. Represented by the first element in the botanical name.

GLOCHID: tuft of bristly hairs on the areole.

HABITAT: natural home of the plant.

HERMAPHRODITE: bisexual; having both male and female parts in a flower.

JOINT: section of stem.

NATURALIZED: referring to plants flourishing away from their natural habitat.

NOCTURNAL: night-flowering.

OFFSET: section of plant capable of rooting.

PECTINATE: comb-like.

PENDENT: hanging downwards.

PHOTOSYNTHESIS: production of carbohydrates from carbon dioxide and water using light energy from the sun.

PROSTRATE: lying flat on the ground.

PSEUDOCEPHALIUM: usually a lateral cephalium.

RADIAL SPINES: spines arranged around the edge of the areole.

RIB: sections of the stem forming raised ridges, usually more or less vertical.

SCALE: thin, leaf-like structure.

SPECIES: an individual plant or closely related group of plants within a genus.

SPINE: thorn-like modified leaf.

SUCCULENT: plant which stores water in its fleshy stems or leaves.

TUBERCLE: small, wart-like swelling or growth.

INDEX